Irma Jepsen
Memorial
Fund

Praise for *Fires in the Bathroom*

"In this book, students get a rare opportunity to voice their opinions about what works and what doesn't in the classroom."
— *Los Angeles Times*

"[Turns] the tables on adults and tells them how to do their jobs."
— The *New York Times*

"This book turns the student-teacher relationship upside down. . . . The bits of advice suggest ways to deepen the unspoken bond between students and teachers."
— *Chicago Tribune*

Praise for *Fires in the Middle School Bathroom*

"This book brings out the essence of what, and how, middle school kids think. Teachers can learn from them—not just new teachers, but those who have been in the field for a while."
— Deborah Kasak, executive director,
     National Forum to Accelerate Middle-Grades Reform

Fires in Our Lives

Fires in Our Lives

Advice for Teachers from Today's High School Students

Kathleen Cushman

Kristien Zenkov

Meagan Call-Cummings

and the youth of What Kids Can Do

THE
NEW
PRESS

NEW YORK
LONDON

© 2021 by What Kids Can Do, Inc.

Requests for permission to reproduce selections from
this book should be made through our website:
https://thenewpress.com/contact.

Published in the United States by The New Press, New York, 2021
Distributed by Two Rivers Distribution

ISBN 978-1-62097-543-5 (hc)
ISBN 978-1-62097-544-2 (ebook)
CIP data is available

The New Press publishes books that promote and enrich public discussion and understanding of the issues vital to our democracy and to a
more equitable world. These books are made possible by the enthusiasm
of our readers; the support of a committed group of donors, large and
small; the collaboration of our many partners in the independent media
and the not-for-profit sector; booksellers, who often hand-sell New Press
books; librarians; and above all by our authors.

www.thenewpress.com

Book design and composition by Sandra Delany
This book was set in Scala and Scala Sans
Printed in the United States of America

10 9 8 7 6 5 4 3 2 1

To the young people coming of age in the midst of crisis

and the teachers who are learning with them

Contents

Preface   xi

Part I. What Makes School Matter

Introduction: Our Lives Have Changed   2

1. At Risk, Together   9

2. Seeking a Way to Belong   19

3. Crossing Our Borders   34

4. Departing from a Single Story   55

5. Finding Our Strengths, Discovering a Purpose   69

6. How Will We Matter?   83

Part II. What Youth Can Do

Overview: Youth Can Make Change   96

Briefing 1. Youth Action on Climate Change   108

Briefing 2. Youth Action on Violence in Their Communities   118

Briefing 3. Youth Action on Voter Engagement   131

Briefing 4. Youth Action on Immigration   147

Briefing 5. Youth Action on Gender Identities   159

Acknowledgments   172

Youth Contributors   175

Notes   177

Resources   181

Index   186

Preface

Just as we sent this book to the publisher, the ground collapsed beneath a generation of adolescent youth. The swiftly growing pandemic of COVID-19 brought unimaginable changes—mass closings of schools and workplaces, mandates to shelter in place, social distancing regulations. On the eve of the November 2020 elections, it had caused well over a million deaths worldwide. U.S. outbreaks numbered more than 8 million cases and 220,000 deaths, with a new surge of infections under way. With the prospect of far more casualties to come, the nation's economy plunged, raising the specter of another Great Depression.

Even before the novel coronavirus swept across the globe, the youth who contributed to this book were voicing the anxieties and inequities of our time. They worried about their families' health and welfare. Dreaming of where their interests might take them, they knew the dice were loaded in favor of those with privilege. They wished schoolwork would connect more directly with their lived experiences. They wanted to make a difference in all these areas—and they hoped their teachers would listen and lend a hand. The pandemic only amplified those concerns.

During lengthy school shutdowns that followed throughout 2020, these youth were navigating an improvisatory patchwork of distance learning, against a daily backdrop of crisis and fear. With this book already in press, we used video calls to reconnect with many of them. As the whole world staggered from this blow, what did they especially need from teachers?

For some, virtual learning had made schoolwork less interesting than ever. Without the social aspects of high school, they lost their impetus to engage. But others had teachers who brought them together in teams. Like expert coaches, they adjusted targets, customized practice, and adapted assessment to their players' readiness. Personal contacts and connections made the biggest difference, students told us. One school began each day with individual online check-ins, inviting students to communicate about their situation with the staff member of their choice. And across the subject areas, many teachers were framing critical skills—mathematical modeling, scientific investigation, artistic expression—as a way to explore essential questions in the context of life and death. They knew that their students were asking, "Why does this matter for us—*now?*"

And then, in late May of 2020, even more hell broke loose. A series of shameful killings of Black people by police and others sparked nationwide street protests of extraordinary scope and scale. Furious and frustrated, young people joined the demonstrations even if they had no connection with activist organizations. One senior organizer from the national activist group Community Change described them as "an army of young people who are more fired up, more pissed off, more ready to be in your face to fix this system than we were five years ago."[1]

In these days, we are continuing to listen to young people and sharing their voices in our videoconferences with educators. What they are saying largely echoes what they told us before the pandemic and the groundswell of civic rage. The same big issues that had been shaping their lives—race and power, identity and potential, aspiration and opportunity, work and pleasure, privacy and public life, risk and protection—now feel ever more pressing as their future grows more uncertain.

Youth continue to tell us that school still matters most when it gives them the sense of belonging, through supportive relationships with teachers as well as peers. More than ever, they want to learn more, to speak out, and to act. And they are hoping that you will stick with them, hearing what they say in the pages that follow, as well as in the years that lie ahead.

Part I | What Makes School Matter

Introduction: Our Lives Have Changed

"Play the role of influencer—it's an even bigger role than a teacher."

1. At Risk, Together

"School's just a small part of a big world where a lot of bad things are going on."

2. Seeking a Way to Belong

"You feel unsteady, like you don't know yourself."

3. Crossing Our Borders

"The first step: seek out people who are very different from you."

4. Departing from a Single Story

"You can't put someone in a box where you think they belong."

5. Finding Our Strengths, Discovering a Purpose

"A teacher can provide the bigger picture we might not get at home."

6. How Will We Matter?

"What if I can only be me? Whatever that is."

Our Lives Have Changed

"Play the role of influencer—it's an even bigger role than a teacher."

T his book came about because the world has changed—and so have the lives of youth.

In 2003, high school students offered advice to their teachers in the first book in this series, *Fires in the Bathroom*. Interviewed by the nonprofit What Kids Can Do (WKCD.org), they described the persistent divide they were experiencing daily in their public schools. Their critique—which boiled down to "My teachers don't understand me"—gave voice to the difference in perspectives between increasingly diverse public school students and the mostly young, middle-class, white, well-intentioned females who stood at the front of their classrooms.[2]

The suggestions of those students still ring true, providing helpful approaches to knowing adolescents better and creating environments that inspire their learning. Seventeen years later, however—a lifetime for those interviewed in this volume—an avalanche of change has roared across the social and emotional landscape of youth. In every area from climate change to communications, volatile developments are affecting them in new and often troubling ways.

At school and in their neighborhoods, they navigate environments marked by divisive rhetoric and cultural clashes. An unrelenting flood of social media has a huge effect on how others see them and how they see themselves. In the larger world that awaits them, existential threats loom large. No wonder teachers are witnessing an unprecedented level of anxiety in their students.

In our extended interviews with some sixty U.S. youth, we found that they want something more from teachers now. In addition to support for academics, they need skills that will help them survive the new "fires" that threaten to overwhelm their lives.

Whether they are studying the U.S. Constitution or analyzing the pH of water, they want to focus on the present danger and the perilous future. They gravitate to history and science, literature and art that resonates with their states of mind. They want inspiring examples of action in times of great crisis. And they want to take their own learning into their communities.

Teachers, too, are reaching for support. How can they cover the required curriculum while focusing on the issues that threaten society? How can they teach through controversy while maintaining respectful norms? Somehow they have to fulfill their academic obligations by discovering what matters most to their adolescent students and by building substantive knowledge and skills that will matter to them. This book aims to give some ideas about how to do that.

OUR STUDENTS HAVE CHANGED

For over a year, we three researchers—each of us long committed to raising youth voices—went out to gather insights from a new generation. Seeking diversity as well as depth in our interviews for the first six chapters, we spoke at length with close to fifty students from public high schools that we already knew well from our prior work. For the issue-related "briefings" in the second part of the book, we also sought out more than a dozen young people who were taking action with local or national youth initiatives.

- Kathleen Cushman interviewed public school students in New York City and Oakland, California, and contacted young activists in Arizona, Massachusetts, Michigan, New Jersey, Ohio, and Utah.

- Kristien Zenkov interviewed youth in a high-poverty neighborhood of Cleveland, Ohio; a rural Indiana district with right-wing politics and rock-bottom school funding; and two Northern Virginia high schools with high levels of diversity and transiency.

- Meagan Call-Cummings interviewed youth from well-established, white farm families and newly arrived migrant families in rural Idaho, and others from a highly diverse suburban Northern Virginia high school.

Our choices reflect the fact that the student body profile of U.S. public high schools has changed dramatically since 2003, when this Fires series of youth voices first began. In 2017, according to the National Center for Education Statistics (NCES), groups of young people previously classified as minority students in the United States were on the cusp of becoming the majority: 51 percent white, 24 percent Hispanic, 16 percent Black, 5 percent Asian/Pacific Islander, 3 percent multiracial, and 1 percent American Indian/Alaskan Native. Regional distinctions had shifted, too. Minority populations, while still concentrated in urban areas and the South, had also increased in traditionally homogeneous (mostly white) areas outside of cities, introducing new groups of students into suburban public school systems.[3]

Language diversity rides on these coattails. By fall 2015, U.S. public schools enrolled nearly 5 million English language learners (ELLs), roughly 9.5 percent of their students. California had the highest percentage; in 2015, more than 1.3 million ELL students amounted to 21 percent of the state's public elementary and secondary school enrollment. In seven other states—Nevada, Texas, New Mexico, Colorado, Alaska, Kansas, and Washington—English learners constituted 10 percent or more of the student body. Roughly three-quarters of students with limited English proficiency said they spoke Spanish as their primary language at home. The remainder spoke a wide variety of languages, including Arabic, Chinese, and Vietnamese. In Maine, Somali was the most common language English learners spoke at home. In Vermont, it was Nepali.

How students feel about high school often turns on what they think of their teachers. They pick up cues that signal respect and rapport, and they notice when teachers make false assumptions. Color, ethnicity, gender, language, culture, and various other personal characteristics can build bridges—or unintended barriers—in a high school classroom.

Despite the change in student demographics in the past decade, teacher demographics have remained largely unchanged. In 2017, 82 percent of public school teachers were white, 6.8 percent Black, and 7.8 percent Hispanic (NCES). Concerted efforts to enlist and welcome a more diverse workforce of teachers have yet to alter the face of who leads most U.S. classrooms today.

Not surprisingly, research indicates that students are more likely to succeed in school when their teachers have similar cultural identities. A "mismatch" of understanding and shared values may negatively affect students who differ culturally from their mostly white teachers. Racial attitudes can also affect school discipline. In studies that control for student behavior, Black and Latinx students are still three to six times more likely than their white peers to be suspended from school.[4]

This cultural and racial mismatch also takes a toll on teachers. During the 2015–2016 school year, 10 percent of teachers reported feeling threatened by a student at their school (NCES) and 6 percent reported that they had been physically attacked by a student. Such realities contribute not just to teacher dissatisfaction and burnout, but to a newly documented phenomenon—teacher "demoralization"—where educators feel that external factors increasingly deny them the ability to do "good" work.[5]

Chastening, as well, is the uptick in mood disorders that students carry to school. Thirty-one percent of teens in a recent survey by the American Psychological Association said they had felt overwhelmed by stress during the previous month. Those age fifteen to twenty-one reported experiencing the most stress of any age group on issues of immigration policy, sexual harassment, climate change, mass shootings, and suicide.[6] Diagnoses of anxiety, the leading cause of disruption to young adult mental health, shot up 20 percent from 2007 to 2012 among children ages six to seventeen.[7] A Johns Hopkins study found that in 2014, 11.3 percent of adolescents reported major depression, up from 8.7 percent ten years earlier. In 2015, the suicide rate for teenage girls reached a forty-year high.[8] In an online survey by Pew Research Center in late 2018, 70 percent of respondents ages thirteen to seventeen said they saw anxiety and depression as a major problem among their peers.[9]

The rise of social media, many argue, has fueled the current decline in adolescent mental health. Young people are spending more time with technology than they do with any other activity outside of school,[10] a cause for concern. Less understood are the ways their online activities often meld with their in-school social lives, overlapping and unfolding simultaneously during the school day[11] and influencing students' emotional, social, and academic behaviors in real time.

THE SUPPORT OUR TEACHERS NEED

Recognizing such "fires" in their students' lives, teachers rightly ask how they can make a difference. As examples throughout this book illustrate, every school has good teachers doing good work—both in their content areas and in social and emotional areas. By integrating behavioral and academic skills, they are fostering the connection and self-reflection on which deeper learning depends.[12]

These teacher practices mirror the research on student-centered learning. Prosocial purpose, for example, has particular significance during the teenage years, we have learned.[13] When teachers help students improve noncognitive skills such as self-regulation, they raise both grades and the likelihood of completing high school, more than do teachers who help students improve standardized test scores.[14] Early warning and college readiness indicators that identify struggling students early in their secondary school education support the goal of all students graduating from high school.[15]

Yet teachers also remind us that "what works" cannot take hold unless the system stands behind it. Too often, their superiors undermine new practices both directly and indirectly. Teachers offer many examples—some bureaucratic, some more personal—of how their efforts shrivel and die:

- Insufficient time for teachers to plan thoughtful work together and to learn and practice ways to continually improve
- Policies that track, flunk, and suspend students
- Punitive, no-compromise approaches to the mistakes that students make
- Tolerating the bad-mouthing of youth by adults in the school.

To surmount such obstacles, teachers develop ways to support each other as well as their students. They work within their locus of control, but also seek out allies in the system and beyond. In the classroom, teachers trying to do "good work" aim to know all their students well enough to keep them going despite setbacks. "Don't assess in ways that extinguish hope!" one veteran teacher warned. "If someone receives a zero for not turning in an assignment, that person cannot recover to a passing average."

With allies up the bureaucratic ladder, such ground-level teacher wisdom may help shape district or state policy. Chicago's public school district, for example, has adopted early warning and college readiness indicators that identify struggling high school students in time to provide them with extra support.[16] Many of the schools represented in this book have pioneered practices that spread to larger networks. Even as the contexts of instruction adapted to the pandemic, teachers were forging new approaches to serve youth in times of crisis.

In our first six chapters, nearly four dozen adolescents in many different settings describe the fault lines that are sending deep tremors through the landscape of their lives. They realize that their generation will disproportionately bear the consequences of that shifting ground. They hope that school can help them and worry that it will not. As tectonic changes—political, cultural, social, and personal—alter the trajectories of their lives, these young people are finding ways to take action in the larger world.

The second half of this book presents five "briefings" on issues that ignite such action: climate change, community violence, voter engagement, immigration, and gender identities. Each briefing includes substantial first-person perspectives by youth whose passion, pragmatism, and commitment bring the issue into sharp relief. And each briefing offers a curated sampler of actionable materials on its subject, from a wealth of resources developed by educators and nonprofit initiatives who make their work available in the public domain.

Both inside our schools and in the greater community, this book attempts to document how young people become adults, with the support of trusted adults. Liam, at sixteen, captures it in a nutshell. "Play the role of influencer," he said. "It's an even bigger role than a teacher."

At Risk, Together

"School's just a small part of a big world where a lot of bad things are going on."

Two factors—risk and safety—come up repeatedly as the students in these pages speak to teachers about their lives and their learning. Although their stories differ in the particulars, they suggest a generational pattern shaped by new and escalating threats. And the tensions that are shifting the course of young people inevitably affect their teachers' actions, too.

Youth in this tumultuous era are already experiencing catastrophic changes in the world they will inherit. They are living out the complexities of their origins, genders, and family circumstances. Many are turning to life-threatening behaviors for relief from their anxiety. But they all want to survive and to thrive. And they wish that their teachers could help.

High school teachers, too, describe their work in terms of risk and safety. They feel daily pressure to meet the learning needs of very different students in very large numbers. They have scant time to collaborate with colleagues. Student scores on standardized tests affect teacher evaluations, so they focus on what's tested. Besieged by competing expectations, many feel drained and devalued.

Teachers and students are at risk, together—and both depend on the actions of the other. When adolescents share what's going on with them, they help teachers in "doing school" effectively. And as young people see that adults are listening, their own minds also open. Both parties can start to generate important questions—ones that arise from real tensions—and connect with both academic work and the world beyond school.

Taken seriously, that process shapes a learner's experience in lasting ways:

- It connects the academic curriculum with the social and emotional needs of learners.

- It equips learners to explore essential questions in a world at risk. (Is health care a human right? Should people have to pay for higher education? How might capitalism affect climate change?)

- It includes learners' insights and actions in assessments of their academic and personal progress.

The high school youth featured in these pages tell of their needs, their questions, and their hopes and fears as they make their way through these tumultuous times. Each of the following sections offers a preview of what students will bring up in the chapters ahead. Their stories share a common thread: Teachers can make a difference.

SEEKING A WAY TO BELONG

In Oakland, California, Hoda struggled to reconcile her dream of studying government at Stanford with her Sunni Muslim family's expectation that she would soon enter an arranged marriage. By eleventh grade, she had set her heart on future freedoms—but she also felt that the larger community viewed her as an outsider. "I see what's going on in the government," she said, "and I want more people like me to have a voice. Being Muslim, I'll have to work ten times harder."

In New York City, Ben had gone to grade school with peers who mostly spoke Spanish, and his large public high school had only a small minority of white students like him. Across cultures, he found friends who shared his affinity for using mordant humor to defang hostility and relieve anxiety. "My friends of color might throw a joke about me carrying a gun to shoot up the school, because I'm white," Ben said.

At fifteen, Shelby had not yet come out to her multigenerational African American family in Harlem, but she identified as queer at school. At a neighborhood center for youth like her, she found important ways to both belong and contribute. "I identify with multiple communities," she said, "and I need them as much as they need me."

CROSSING OUR BORDERS

In his midwestern rural community, Liam, fifteen, had absorbed the religious, economic, and cultural conservatism of his white, Christian family. At the same time, he was exploring the tensions of his own identity. He believed that his parents had earned their comfortable circumstances, yet he yearned for a creative future in a big city like Chicago or New York. And although he took pride

---

Scouting the Borders

As young people imagine the possible terrain of their futures, talking about those unacknowledged borders—especially race, class, faith, and gender stereotyping—may help them to cross those borders safely. For example, new perspectives could emerge in small-group discussions in which students think about what "success" entails, in an area of interest to them:

- Create a picture (in words or images) of a role that interests you.

- What expectations or barriers might you encounter in achieving that role?

- What support would you need to reach that role? Where might you look for that support?

- Imagine yourself in that role. What do you think would most satisfy you?

- What drawbacks might come along with working in that role? How do you imagine dealing with those drawbacks?

---

in excelling at school, he felt stigmatized by peers for his unusual interests and ambitions.

When youth described the lines that separated them, race and ethnicity came up often. The third child of Liberian immigrants, Jeffrey grew up in suburban Virginia with few Black peers. By senior year, he had checked off all the boxes of high achievement and was applying to top universities. But he remained acutely aware of how others stereotyped him: "This kid is ghetto."

Old constraints on gender roles also showed up—in big ways and small. Kate, whose parents were Muslim and Hindu, noticed that her Northern Virginia high school's dress codes had much stricter rules for female students. "Even if we are in this very progressive new generation where men and women are equal," Kate said, "in the back of our heads there's a subconscious, 'Oh, it's okay if he wears that.'"

DEPARTING FROM A SINGLE STORY

When Angel was nine, he lived in a New York City homeless shelter, where he cared for three younger brothers and his single father, an invalid. At sixteen, he credited both his supportive fourth-grade teacher and his dedicated foster father for turning his life around. Outgoing and voluble, Angel learned to love debating as much as basketball, and he liked to point out their similarities. Dreaming of a career in journalism, he produced a vlog on his smartphone that featured commentary and satirical interviews with peers.

Growing up in Cleveland, Kynedy wished her teachers knew how much she needed them to reverse the low expectations she faced at home—"people saying 'you can't do that' or 'you're not going to be this.'" She needed a plan, Kynedy said, if she was to get the help she needed.

Jennifer, whose parents came from Guatemala to Northern Virginia, knew that her extended family depended on her education. When her grandfather was dying of pancreatic cancer, she had to educate herself "on how to educate them." She felt doubly stung by their doubts that she would achieve her ambitious goals.

Rekik, at sixteen, also chafed at the ways that adults tried to categorize her. Her parents had come to Northern Virginia from Ethiopia four years before, and she resisted their expectation that she would excel in a scientific or tech career.

Find Out What Matters to Youth

Sometimes we're not even learning. We're just trying to pass and move on to the next curriculum. I would like that to change. – JENNIFER

What the teacher was sharing felt just useless to me. I raised my hand, and I asked, "So . . . what are we learning?" She got really offended—she pulled me back after class and said, "Maggie, you just cannot ask that." If the teacher can't explain, then I don't know what we're doing. – MAGGIE

The difficult issues of our times relate to every academic subject. From the first day of class, you can ask students *what* they're thinking about and also *why* they care. You, too, can reflect on your priorities and how those connect with theirs. Referring back to those reflections as students work with content reminds them how their learning can make a difference.

QUESTIONS FOR STUDENTS

- What do you worry about when you think about your future?
- What personal goals do you have for the future you imagine?
- What connections can you see between your personal goals and the work of this class?

QUESTIONS FOR TEACHERS

- What's your one big goal, as a teacher in this class?
- Based on your students' answers above, what are their most important goals in life?
- Draw connection-lines between your class work and their goals.

Her teachers were also seeing "just one layer," she believed. She wanted them to look closer—but not too close. "School's just a small part of a big world where a lot of bad things are going on," Rekik said.

Rowdy, a ninth grader in rural Idaho, knew he would face a yawning economic and cultural divide when he graduated from high school. "It's gonna take a small miracle to get out from farming, or being a teacher, in this depressing small town," he said, "and instead to live somewhere you want to be."

For some youth, just surviving provided a reason to build new strengths. Rose's mother had fled Mexico after enduring serious sexual harassment in the workplace. In Oakland at eighteen, Rose worried about that happening to her, too. "It can be really scary going into a workplace for the first time and having these men think they can control you," she said. "I don't want to go through that."

Marsela and her younger brother were born in the United States, but their parents were undocumented immigrants from Albania. In grade eleven, she watched with horror as deportation and parent-child separations dominated the news. "I had to sit down with my parents and talk about who's going to stay with me if they got deported," Marsela said.

HELP US TO MATTER

As youth experience the anxieties of these times, the stakes are also rising for their teachers. They, too, may feel at risk in their communities if they incorporate polarizing societal challenges in the work of the classroom. And with numerous classes and up to hundreds of students each day, how can they possibly respond to the "new fires" in their students' lives?

Students speak to that question in the chapters that follow. Above all, they ask their teachers to connect learning with the world that they are navigating. They want to think through complicated issues and discover common ground, where possible. They want to act as resources to each other, as they build new

Learning from a World of Crises

Exploring difficult issues can help youth build a sense of purpose and believe in their own capacity to contribute something of value. This classroom or advisory exercise starts with events in the news. Students collaborate on a shared inquiry with three steps:

- **What?** Students share what they know about the news event. What have they heard? What have they seen? Where is the information coming from? What questions do they have about what occurred? What are the perspectives of those involved? To establish a common understanding of the event (from multiple perspectives, if available), they all peruse the same article, video, or other resource.

- **So what?** Students make sense of the event for themselves, acknowledging that their peers may have different interpretations. What impact does this event have on them personally? Within their broader communities? Throughout the country or the world? What concerns does it raise? What other questions remain for students?

- **Now what?** Students consider how to respond to the event, again acknowledging that their peers may have different opinions. How could individual students, or the group, share their feelings about the event or take action in response? What do they see as possible next steps?

Resources commonly used with this exercise include the *New York Times'* Learning Network, Teaching Tolerance (tolerance.org), and CNN Student News Daily Discussion. Thanks to teachers at the Parker Essential School (Devens, Massachusetts) for this version.

understanding. They want to learn in their communities as well as in their schools. They want—in their imperiled lifetime—to help make a better world.

For example, when she participated in a civic education nonprofit in New York, Scott learned to take part in difficult political conversations across the divide of race. Occasionally she asks a white person: "Would you want to be Black in America?" They always hesitate, she noticed, and then say they're happy with the skin they have. "But I know why they don't want to be Black, and they know, too," says Scott. "In this society, in general it's not good."

Kate had been "the only brown kid" at her elementary and middle schools near the nation's capital. When she started at a very diverse high school with a special biotechnology program, it felt "mind-opening," she said. "So many different cultures, and so many different people, and so many different ideas!"

Given the challenges of poverty, racism, and segregation, Kyle didn't expect to do well at his public high school in Cleveland. In middle school, to avoid being bullied, he had pretended not to care. But by grade ten he had developed a new philosophy rooted in his Black identity. "When Black people get caught up in everybody else's problems, I'm always thinking, 'Focus on you.' If you can't help yourself, you're not going to help others."

In their very different school and community contexts, all these youth wanted their teachers to support and believe in them. "Our education will get us out of this town," declared Rowdy, determined to find his way from rural Idaho into the larger world. In New York City, Kaitlyn took that statement even further. High school teachers who serve as models and mentors, she said, matter now more than ever.

"Our student body, we all have different backgrounds," she said. "But in this school, it's like growing up in the same place. Because of our deep connections with our teachers, we're able to see how they managed to get here. Their different aspects and ideas, as a staff, help us see our possible different avenues of life."

What's Making Us Worry?

Shelby, fifteen, had a cousin whose face bore scars from a gang-related incident. Now she feared for her older brother, in his final year of high school.

> It's dangerous to be Black and walk around our neighborhoods at night. Just because of who you are and how you present yourself, people think that you're dangerous, that you're going to steal from them. My grandmother doesn't let any of us wear hoodies, because of what happened to Trayvon Martin. We could get shot. — SHELBY

Jeremy, at sixteen, worried about the ethics of the ever-advancing science of genetics. In his view, it risked breaching barriers that he regarded as sacred.

> It feels like we're now getting to the point of exploring a realm that shouldn't be controlled by humans. To me, it seems morally wrong to change things in your genes. — JEREMY

Fowler felt that school signaled its mistrust of students as soon as they entered the building.

> Going through the metal detector, we have to take off our shoes, our hairpins, our belts. The security guards get angry with us for not being fast enough. Listen, I've never been a bad kid, I make good choices all the time. But that makes me want to act out. — FOWLER

Marsela wished that her social studies class would draw attention to the successive waves of immigration that shaped United States history from its start.

> For me, it's hardest when people minimize the feelings that come with deportation. Instead of thinking, "There's a reason why they risked everything to come here," they say, "It can't be that bad to go back where you came from." They don't acknowledge that, unless you're Native American, we're all immigrants. — MARSELA

(continued)

What's Making Us Worry? *(continued)*

Jennifer was among many students who described caring for their friends in emotional crises. By grade eleven, that took its toll on her own mental and physical health.

> I hit rock bottom. I needed to take care of myself. Now, moving forward, I can see what's important to me and what is more important.
> — JENNIFER

When Kyle started high school, he didn't expect to do well.

> In my middle school, it wasn't cool to care about school stuff. You would get bullied if it looked like you did. So I had to stop caring, and I wasn't really on track when I came here. — KYLE

As the daughter of Mexican immigrants, Rose also could not stop thinking of children separated from their families at the border.

> People come here to be free, but you hear the news, you see what's going on, people held against their will. It's starting to feel like we're not that free. — ROSE

CHAPTER 2

Seeking a Way to Belong

"You feel unsteady, like you don't know yourself."

Young people discover their sense of self and safety in places where they feel that they belong. At home, in friendship groups, and at school, they continually seek that safety, navigating the tensions that threaten its fragile balance.

In the inevitable ups and downs of adolescence, they are often conveying spoken or unspoken signals to the adults in their lives. If conflict or trauma is heightening their anxiety, they need even more for those people to notice. But often they waver—wanting to talk to a caring adult, yet not wanting to unmask themselves.

Without such help, youth come up with their own ways to cope. Rekik, for example, moved from Ethiopia in seventh grade to join her divorced father in the United States. Four years later, she said she had learned to "find comfort in uncomfortable situations."

> You put me somewhere weird, I'll try to make a bubble. Maybe I'll lock myself in my own head, or maybe I'll talk with somebody to make myself comfortable. — REKIK

Teachers witness behaviors like this all day, every day. When they support those students in finding a way to belong, they are making an important statement: it's normal—not "weird"—to need help on that journey.

> Friends are a great source as well, but I think a trusted adult is better, because they probably have been through the same situations, or know similar ones. — JENNIFER

The expectations of their families shape the experiences of students, as every teacher knows. Some students sense that their families are counting on them to right the wrongs they have encountered, or to ease their economic and psychic woes.

Such pressure weighed on Kate, who had transferred in grade eleven to a specialty biotechnology program in Northern Virginia. Her immigrant parents— one from Trinidad and Tobago, the other from Bangladesh—expected her to excel. As she looked to her future, Kate felt the strain of living up to their hopes.

> My mom never got to finish high school. My dad graduated college, but he doesn't work in a high-paying job—he manages a Papa John's. Both my parents are pushing me really hard to do better, go to a good college, and get a good job. It's just really hard to live up to. – KATE

Jennifer's parents, also immigrants, had not graduated from high school. She knew that they expected her to make a generations-long leap forward in academic achievement.

> I was raised in an environment where you can't waste time. You're always active: working, studying, or doing something involving the community. Sitting and watching TV with my family—that's considered lazy, we don't tolerate that. I think a lot about not disappointing my parents in that tradition of my culture. – JENNIFER

Emily's mother, who came from Guatemala, made clear how much her children's education mattered in the land of opportunity.

> Her mindset is "You have to do your best, there is no second place." If she could overcome her hardships, then we can overcome whatever we are going through. It's just a lot of pressure. – EMILY

School and Family Can Bring the Pieces Together

A teacher's empathic connection with a student in need can reverberate for years. For some time before he entered middle school, Angel and his three younger siblings lived in a New York City shelter. At seventeen, successful in school and sports, he wrote this account of how the attention of his fourth- and fifth-grade teacher and his foster father brought him to young adulthood.

My childhood was pretty much gone, when I had Ms. Rojas as my teacher for two years. My mom and dad had separated—to this day I honestly don't know where she is. My dad was really sick with his diabetes, and he couldn't work or make rent payments. We were evicted from our home and had to apply for a shelter. I had to step up my role for my three younger siblings. I remember using the stove at nine, ten years old, cooking rice and beans and spaghetti.

Ms. Rojas would always talk to me during lunch and I used to tell her about my situation. I saw her as a mentor, someone I could trust. That year for Christmas, she bought me a whole bunch of Transformer toys. I came home to the shelter with this huge bag, kind of like Santa. She made our Christmas that year.

We were all put in foster care at the same time, and my brother Joshua and I were separated from our two younger siblings. I used to cry every night. My foster dad would tell me, "Just look at this as your second chance at life." I was young, so I didn't really process that. Then, out of nowhere, he moved us into a four-bedroom apartment upstairs. When my fifth-grade graduation came around, he picked us up in the van, and I turned around and saw my youngest siblings. He said, "This is your gift for graduation—they live with us now!" We actually all got adopted, and now we call him Dad.

In my birth family, no one went past tenth grade, and I'm a senior. Now it's my turn to do what I have to do. Every night now, it's us four siblings and my dad. We pray, then we eat dinner together, talking about everyone's day. We can talk about anything and be fine. Even though we argue about any little thing, we accept our differences. That contributes to building a founda-tion—a bond within and outside the home, a trusting relationship. – ANGEL

But in addition to feeling the familiar pressure to do well, young people may also be worrying about circumstances at home. Inevitably—and often invisibly—that affects their lives at school.

At fifteen, Kaidyan played an important role in his multigenerational African American household. In ninth grade, he would leave their house in Brooklyn at six in the morning to walk his sister to kindergarten, then travel an hour by subway to his school in Manhattan.

> There's all those gangs around and something happens every day. A friend of mine got stabbed—that could've been me. But I prioritize what I have to take care of, and I have a group of people that make sure they know I'm okay. My grandmother's like, "Why didn't you call me when you reached the school?" — KAIDYAN

Marsela was making her own contingency plans in case her undocumented parents were deported. Distant relatives in the area might agree to take her if that happened, but she dreaded the disruption of her family. Wistfully, she imagined taking over her father's job as superintendent of the small New York City apartment building where they lived.

> I could take out the garbage after school, to support me and my brother. — MARSELA

Even in a strained situation, young people want and need to belong in a supportive family. Miledy, whose parents are farm workers in Idaho, will be the first in the family to graduate from high school. When she developed an eating disorder, they stood by her.

> I felt ugly, worthless. My grades were going down, and I just wanted to be alone. My parents tried to be there for me, but I just pushed them away. When I got help, they showed me even more love. — MILEDY

When tensions flared with her mother, Kate would lock herself in her bedroom until her father came home.

Sometimes she'll scream at me for little things, and I can't do anything, so I isolate myself. If my dad's in the room, he kinda calls her out when she does that, but I can't. — KATE

Roxy's parents had divorced seven years earlier. In high school, she was still balancing their competing needs and priorities.

It's still really tricky for me, weighing whose feelings are going to get hurt in which situations. Something might make my father mad, but my mother really happy. — ROXY

Immigrant parents like hers, Jennifer noticed, had apprehensions about whether the school community welcomed them. She wished her school would reach out with workshops and activities to get to know them better.

Teachers might not know a family's lifestyle, or their struggles with the language, or how different our school system is from what they knew before. — JENNIFER

Aside from taking over her father's job as the building super, Marsela saw school as her only chance if her parents had to leave. After college, she was hoping to go into politics. When her social studies teacher took up the nation's history of immigration, Marsela's interest spiked. "It's the subject that's affected me the most," she said.

A PLACE AMONG PEERS

Outside the realm of family, youth seek another proving ground in their friendship groups. At school, teachers often observe them trying to find their place among their peers.

Students recognize that need, too. As Shannon watched his Oakland schoolmates flaunt their upscale belongings, he saw it as an effort to belong.

> People like to stunt or flex at school, like show off something new they got. It's like they have this fear that they won't be accepted or someone is going to judge or bully them. – SHANNON

Constructing a facade takes its toll, Rowdy observed. Although others in his rural Idaho school regarded him as an extrovert, he saw himself as a chameleon.

> I am the nerdy kid, the quiet kid, the loud kid, the go-getter kid, the teacher's pet, I guess you could say, the attention-seeker, the smart kid. I put on all these facades—this shell of "Hey, how *you* doin'?" When really it just exhausts me, emotionally and socially, to talk to people. – ROWDY

School can provide a middle ground to youth, where they can explore possible new identities. Monse, who went to school with Rowdy, began to diversify her friendships in eleventh grade.

> I can be with whoever I want, however I am. It's cool. You just have to learn to be yourself, without caring so much about what they think. – MONSE

In turn, Monse reached out to Miledy, who was struggling with her eating disorder. Their friendship made all the difference, Miledy said.

> High school was really hard for me in the beginning and I couldn't talk to anyone. When my grades were going down, and I just couldn't do it anymore, Monse would talk me through what I could do better, for myself. We also went to a retreat with our church, and that helped both of us. – MILEDY

As they mature and change, young people may also part ways from their schoolmates. Tanner, whose Mormon family also lived in rural Idaho, was bullied by peers in grades seven and eight. "I felt disconnected from myself," he said. In high school, he decided to risk sitting at different tables in the lunchroom.

Finding the Words for Our Emotions

It takes practice to put one's feelings into words, and high school teachers can help their students get better at that skill. As adolescents learn to identify and describe emotions in different academic contexts, they also expand their range of expression in their personal lives. For example:.

- Studying literary or historical texts, students can speculate on the feelings and motivations of characters or people described.

- In science, they can explore the biology and psychology of emotions such as happiness, anger, sadness, fear, surprise, and disgust.

- In math, they can consider whether anxiety and other emotions affect attitudes toward mathematical reasoning or problem solving.

- In advisory groups, they can learn to listen to peers, verify what they intended to say, and actively build upon what they hear, building new understanding of what others and they themselves are feeling.

Many social and emotional learning (SEL) programs help youth explore conflict and cooperation by finding more specific language to describe their feelings. "Emotion wheels" in lovely colors go beyond the lingo of "mad, sad, glad, bad" to reach more accurate and nuanced descriptions of emotional states.

You feel unsteady, like you don't know yourself. But you can't just hide and do nothing. The more you talk to people, the more you recognize what you like and go for it. I like band, I like gaming club, studying World War Two is awesome. And you can strive to be better. It feels good. When other people know that, you can all of a sudden see who you are. – TANNER

Once youth recognize their preconceptions about others, they can decide whether to accept or reject those assumptions. That process—which sometimes involves forgiving themselves, or their peers, for whatever they thought—also helps them find ways to open up to others.

In New York City, Kaitlyn observed a classmate doing just that.

> In class, she would go to different tables, while I would just stay in my place, talking to the same people every day. At first I thought, "Why is she trying to get to know these people?" But I overheard their conversations, and it was really profound. That helped me open up and find empathy for others, trying to get to know them. – KAITLYN

Maggie had changed schools many times by grade eleven, as her father's naval career took the family to new locations. She viewed that as an asset, compared to friends who had lived a more settled life.

> It scares me that some people just never get outside of their bubble. That's why I want to travel, because a big part of changing yourself for the better is seeing everything that you possibly can—the good and the bad—and then choosing what you like. – MAGGIE

In her Northern Virginia high school, Jennifer had been building bridges between students from different backgrounds. A proud Hispanic student whose parents came from Guatemala, she worked with others to break down barriers through roundtable discussions and peace conferences. She especially sought out experiences that went beyond traditional gender roles.

> In the past women were on the margins and in a box. But now we're trying to break that box and scatter everywhere where we personally identify. – JENNIFER

A TEACHER TO TRUST

For youth who feel isolated and unseen, even one teacher who reaches out can make a big difference.

> Even if you just talk to us about everyday life, it helps to know that your teacher isn't just there to go through the day-to-day trials of school. – CARSON

Natalie, a fifth-year senior in her city's 2,500-student high school, felt unmoored both at school and at home. She wanted to join the military but was struggling to earn her high school diploma first. Her older siblings had moved on, and her divorced mother was planning to remarry.

Sometimes I wish I could have someone to talk to, who could say, "This is wrong" or "This is right." I want to start my life already, but instead I'm back in school doing the same thing. — NATALIE

Help Us Belong, in Your Class and in School

What teachers reveal about themselves—and the tone they use when talking with adolescents—can help students feel more engaged in learning. A teacher's candor creates a classroom community of trust, where it's safe to speak about things that matter. Below, students describe how teachers and administrators help them feel more included and connected.

Find out more about us. Start the course with an activity or assignment where we share any prior experience with the material as well as our interests, concerns, and goals in the class. Make it engaging—and keep it confidential!

You don't need to know every bit of information—the gist of us is fine. — REKIK

Understand and encourage and support what each kid wants to accomplish in their life. — LIAM

Share your own personal stories. It sets a tone of trust when you tell us more about yourself, either in class or in spare moments. If our questions make you uncomfortable, you don't have to share details. "That's not easy to answer," you could say. "Maybe some other time."

We are supposed to see teachers as authority figures, but they're people, too. When everybody is being themselves, it makes school seem less institutionalized. — KYNEDY   *(continued)*

Help Us Belong, in Your Class and in School *(continued)*

Create opportunities for us to share our stories. We may not want to talk about ourselves in class, and we won't want to share everything. But you can give us other opportunities—perhaps by taking photographs of things that matter to us, or writing about something personal.

> This photo shows the hill I walk on to get to and from work. I work full time at the zoo to help out my family. I don't make a lot, but it helps pay for my dad's prescriptions and my own expenses. Every day when I come home from work I walk uphill, and I feel like I'm walking uphill all the time. – LINDSAY

Open doors to our possible futures. We may not know what's out there, or how to access it. A teacher can facilitate our growing knowledge in many ways, from guest speakers to exploratory field trips.

> I told her I wanted to go to Case Western, and she set up a campus tour. I made a whole day out of it. – KYLE

Hire faculty that reflects our diversity. We feel more seen and understood when teachers have experiences in common with our own. Shared factors such as race, ethnicity, language, gender, displacement, or life conditions can give us a sense that we, too, belong in this learning community.

> If you weren't okay in a class, you could connect with her. She would say, "Oh, I went through that, too. I understand."– DYLAN

Kaynna had enrolled in a special biomedical program at a large high school in suburban Virginia. In ninth grade, she was feeling so stressed that she began to shut down. Her history teacher noticed her sleeping in class and referred her to the school counselor.

> I'm glad that she noticed, because a lot of them didn't. I kinda wanted

help, but I was scared to ask. I felt like, what's the point? I'm going to get in trouble for being "not normal." But she would always ask me how I was feeling. She could tell. – KAYNNA

Kaitlyn grew up, she said, in a family that signaled, "If you need to cry, don't let anyone see you." At her very diverse public high school in New York City, supportive teachers helped her open up in times of stress.

In middle school, I would cry in the halls and a teacher would say, "It's going to be okay," and then walk on. Here, a passing teacher will sit down with you and talk. That kind of attention brightens up your whole vision. Just knowing they're there has made me feel stronger—like I'm safe and nestled in this place. – KAITLYN

Adam, brought low by a serious depression in grade ten, appreciated the teacher who noticed his half-joking remarks about self-destructive feelings and then took helpful action.

She really got me, when I was struggling in this dark pit of emotions and I didn't know it myself. I'm not sure where I'd be right now if it hadn't have been for her. – ADAM

Adults at school can also help youth find ways to connect with peers. In the midst of his gender transition, Dylan knew that others, too, were struggling with difficult issues. A staff member he talked with took an interest in the poetry he wrote and asked Dylan to share it at assemblies with peers and their parents.

Kids are so closed off when things happen to each other, whether it's suicide or hurting yourself. And your parents don't know about it. Now I can help people through my words, telling them, "I know what you go through. Life may be hard, but knowing someone's there is always better than doing it by yourself." – DYLAN

Useful Words for Interventions

When adults intervene in social and emotional situations with students, language matters. The right words can help to defuse tension, open a dialogue, or start building a scaffold to help youth address a longstanding challenge. Some examples of wording and actions:

- "I am here for you. You're safe. What can I do to help?"

- "Let's take a walk," or "Let's take a break."

- "Tell me about it."

- "Can you draw it, or write about it?"

- "What does it feel like in your body?"

- "Let's think of some endings for what could happen."

- "What can you do now, to feel better?"

- "Do you want to try a breathing exercise together?" (For example, matching breaths, or "box breathing" to slow down and regulate the breath.)

WAYS YOU CAN BRING US TOGETHER

In any classroom, the dynamics that connect teachers, students, and academic content can make or break the learning process. For example, Milan hated it when behavioral issues took over her classes.

> It's a really thin line. In the middle of class, a teacher might be trying to get someone to calm down, or give them a hug. There has to be, like, a boundary. The perfect mix: a teacher who cares, who's funny and relatable, but also tough. She's telling you, "Be independent." — MILAN

Many students said that they learned more when teachers prioritized developing classroom community. "Even though we're all in a class together," said Roxy, "we can still feel really disconnected."

Take a break from whatever you're teaching, to create space and deconstruct the tension. Incorporate it into your curriculum. Why are we saying these things? How do we feel about each other, as a learning community? – ROXY

In grade twelve at that same school, Miles noted that the faculty treated disagreement as an opportunity for dialogue. His social studies teacher regularly voiced controversial opinions in class, so that students who disagreed would learn to use evidence to support their own ideas.

It's really useful, having a space where students can interact with teachers and see them as people with diverse opinions. – MILES

In a much larger high school, Ben saw his very diverse teachers and schoolmates providing "sort of a new family, if students don't have that acceptance at home."

I have a lot of friends whose family's religions or beliefs can bind them. The Muslim females in my English class talk about how their families want them to focus on marrying a wealthy husband, instead of moving into college. Also, a close friend on my robotics team is openly gay, and he's been fighting that battle with his family. – BEN

Working with youth in extracurricular activities gives teachers another chance to support young people in their connections with peers. As captain of her Idaho school's cheer team, Chloe started a "truth circle" to ease tensions among her Latina and white teammates, who often didn't socialize in other settings.

Some girls are dominant, and others not very sure of themselves. I want everyone to believe in themselves and feel like they're why this team is so good. In the circle, we pass a "spirit stick" and say how we're feeling, good or bad.

Making Your Power Map

A veteran history teacher in New York, Andy Snyder, created this exercise to help students explore how they experience power in their lives. His directions: "Answer these questions as best you can: with single words (maybe a noun, a verb, and an adjective), with names of specific people and places (in and out of school), or with a short anecdote to show (rather than tell) your ideas. If you get stuck, talk to the people next to you. We're figuring this out together."

- What is power? How do you think of it? _____

  _____

- Where and/or when do you feel the most powerful? The most powerless?

  _____

- Who or what has power over you, directly and/or indirectly? _____

  _____

- Who or what do you have power over, directly and/or indirectly?

  _____

- Who do you share power *with* (that is, together you increase your power)?

  _____

- What do you have the power to do? _____

  _____

- In what ways would you like to be more powerful? _____

  _____

(continued)

Making Your Power Map *(continued)*

- Do you think power is distributed like a pyramid, or more like a web? Or like something else? Explain. _____
  _____

- Think about how power flows. Then draw a concept map or an actual map of yourself in a specific space (home, school, the city, the world), including powerful people and other forces that define our possibilities. Relax and let something flow onto the paper.

Hearing others open up makes more people share something. And if things aren't working, we resolve it right then, before it becomes a big issue. – CHLOE

In eleventh grade at her rural Idaho school, Monse found a place to belong on the drama team.

People usually think drama is for weird kids. But they were just so cheerful, like, "I'm going to be me and if you don't accept it, that's your problem." It boosted my confidence so much, even though I was a newbie. – MONSE

In and out of the classroom, the genuine interest and supportive actions of teachers had made an important difference to these students. When her teachers took an open and engaging stance, Emily concluded, she did better.

Some teachers just want to get the job over with: "Here's the information, get out of my class." Others have the attitude, "I am not a babysitter. I'm here to teach you and that's it." But a couple of my teachers definitely put me in the right mindset. I don't voice my problems to them, but they do keep a positive attitude in their class, and that helps me indirectly. – EMILY

For youth who can count on that, their school offers a place they can belong.

CHAPTER 3

Crossing Our Borders

"The first step: seek out people who are very different from you."

Young people continually confront cultural and political borders—in their families and neighborhoods, at their workplaces, on social media, and wherever else they venture. High school itself can feel to them like a tinderbox, stoked by discord they cannot ignore.

Kaynna, a tenth grader at a large suburban high school in Virginia, regarded many everyday interactions as increasingly hurtful. Her father had come from Ethiopia, and she felt alienated when people used divisive labels in conversations about complex issues like immigration.

> I do want to participate and vote. But I don't always agree with what one or the other party is saying. That type of democracy makes people judge someone so quickly. And it's the same for religion and race. – KAYNNA

In grade ten, Liam stayed away from political arguments. His father was a successful entrepreneur, and their family shared the Trump-style conservatism of working-class rural Indiana. Liam viewed those with different political perspectives as merely reacting to their own personal or economic challenges and failures.

> There's probably something going on in their life that they're frustrated with, that they didn't see as going their way, and they need to find someone to blame. – LIAM

Liam and his friends also didn't talk about their religious differences.

Borders and Guides

Students wish their teachers would explicitly acknowledge the tensions of "border lines" that youth are confronting in many different social contexts. This exercise offers one way for youth to enter that conversation and imagine themselves safely crossing such borders.

WHO MATTERS TO ME?

Make a three-column T-chart. In the first column, list the people in your life who matter to you, whom you care about, whom you engage with regularly, or who have some power over you. Also include people you feel you have some control over, or people you take responsibility for.

SIMILARITIES AND DIFFERENCES

For each of those individual people, in the second column of the T-chart, write down ways that you are similar to, and different from, that person. Pay particular attention to beliefs and principles—thinking beyond superficial descriptors (such as hair color, or age).

WHO WOULD MAKE A GOOD "GUIDE"?

In the third column of the T-chart, name someone—in your life, in school, in history, even a celebrity—who you think would have a "middle ground" between your own position and that of each person you named. Who would serve as a good "guide"—so that you and each person you named might cross the borders between your beliefs?

DISCUSSION

Use a "concentric circle" strategy to discuss these individuals, issues, and guides. (Half the class sits in the inner circle, half on the outer circle, each facing a peer.) After talking together, move one person clockwise to talk about another individual or element of your chart.

I have Muslim friends, Catholics, Mormons, atheists. But if you get into these issues, you're not going to get out. I might say something that might offend them, and it just would bring this ugly clash that's going to break up a friendship. — LIAM

Jeremy, whose parents had come from Korea, was feeling the tension between his own new opportunities and his worry about the numbers of other immigrants seeking the same.

My mom feels that we shouldn't limit immigration because America is the land of the free. But I think that we have to start having some limitations, or we will exceed the population our economy can handle. — JEREMY

Youth often echo the larger culture's tendency to discount those whose views differ from theirs. Yet the social relationships of school can also provide powerful leverage for learning to listen. As tensions rose in the worlds they navigated, many of these young people were seeking ways to communicate across their differences.

HOW DIFFERENCE MATTERS

Looking plainly at how those differences arose provides a first step. For example, across the board, students have long heard the message that doing well at school will open the doors to college. They share their families' hopes that their futures will lift their fortunes.

The dream of college as the ultimate equalizer has not materialized in their generation, however. As they saw entrenched inequities block the progress of peers who went before them, students without privilege were absorbing a bitter lesson.

In senior year at her Oakland high school, Nyzja felt overcome by the onslaught of college-related work and deadlines. She dreamed of attending a top state university, but worried whether she could handle the academic workload, the financial burden, and the tensions of racial stereotyping.

My cousins in college talk about their struggles, not having enough money. I'm scared of pushing myself to the point where I break down. And it can be hard having to constantly prove yourself because of your skin color. I've had that before, where people don't think I'm smart or strong enough. – NYZJA

The oldest of six children, Kaynna aspired to a career in medicine. As a Black female at a large suburban Virginia high school, she felt she had to prove herself, and she adjusted how she looked and behaved when she was with peers who looked different from her.

In a way, I feel like I have to closet myself. You have to work ten times harder in school and in life than people that are not the same skin tone as you. But I think that will change when Black people prove themselves. – KAYNNA

Local, state, and national politics all play their parts in shaping equitable opportunities and societal support for youth from any background. That realization led Aissata and Fatoumata, classmates in grade eleven, to volunteer with a New York City nonprofit promoting civic education and youth voter registration.

Too often, Aissata said, schools made it hard for teachers and students to examine their own ideas, as well as those of others.

In some cases, the facts support both sides! We need classroom debates and Socratic circles, where students actually talk about a problem and think for themselves and reach their own conclusions—without being told, "This is right; this is wrong. If you do this, you're in trouble." – AISSATA

Such classroom activities can carry over to community interactions, Fatoumata pointed out.

We've learned to talk about issues to others, based on articles that we read beforehand. You're leading the discussion right then and there, trying to bring your stance into it, and you have to use "accountable talk." You're respectfully disagreeing. – FATOUMATA

Kaitlyn's conservative middle-class parents both came from Mexico, and in grade twelve she, too, was sorting out her own ideas and beliefs. Her history teacher, she said, regularly voiced provocative viewpoints with unpopular reasoning, simply to draw students into discourse on volatile issues.

> It's important to have some sort of foundation: "We agree on a common idea, but we diverge here." I'm still trying to get there. Teachers tell you to be accepting of other people's political ideas—and yeah, it sounds easy to do. My history teacher doesn't tell you to do it—he actively *does* it. – KAITLYN

Political and community discourses will clash, these youth have come to understand. But they have hope for moving those arguments forward. They are developing an awareness not just of what separates them, but also of their own ability to make choices about their own identities and social networks.

Roxy, in grade twelve, spelled out the impact of such efforts—an insight teachers might put to use in classrooms:

> The first step: Seek out people who are very different from you. One of my closest friends, at first he seemed pretentious, like, "I read Nietzsche and I'm too cool for you." But we connected about *Lord of the Rings*. I didn't find out until much later that he was an avid Trump supporter. I asked myself: "Do I really want this friendship?" And the answer was "Yeah, because I do like this person." Anyway, now he's a Communist. – ROXY

WHICH LINES TO CROSS?

Every day at school—and often in every class—adolescents navigate differences within their peer relationships. Some borders they venture across. Some, they approach but never traverse. Others, they defy.

In rural Idaho, Rowdy's eighth-grade teacher paired him in class with a "rich kid" who was slacking off. A good student himself, Rowdy realized that they shared a passion for music and drama.

I would see him sketching in this notebook, but at first he would never show it to me. Inside were all these music notes and prop designs and stage directions. Nobody else at school was into that, so we really bonded over that. — ROWDY

Kyle, a young Black poet at a Cleveland public high school for the arts, knew the lines he would cross and those he would not. When a male peer physically threatened a female classmate, Kyle called him out.

He took her bag and pushed her down. I went and confronted the dude, I got the bag back, and the authorities got involved. My mom thought that it wasn't my problem. But I just can't know that's happening and not do anything about it. I can't just sit. — KYLE

His schoolmate Kynedy, also a poet, learned that finding common ground depended on her approach.

I get in a lot of disagreements with people I'm close to, and I'm a firm believer that every action causes a reaction on the opposite side. Were you going in calmly, or were you being confrontational or violent? — KYNEDY

No matter how their frictions arise—from superficial matters, or in such areas as culture, ethics, or politics—adolescents have a keen awareness of potential hazards. Their desire to "get along" with peers can lead them to avoid conversations that might cause conflict.

As a young person of color in the largest high school in Virginia, Rekik tried to "match, don't clash" with her classmates as she sensed different tensions and expectations.

How I act in English class might not be accepted in my aerospace class, where I'm the only girl. And even with friends, it has to be a give-and-take. You act one way with one person, but with someone else you match her personality so you don't clash. — REKIK

Hoda wanted to confront the stereotypes that her largely Black and Latinx schoolmates in Oakland had about her Arab culture and Muslim faith. When teachers put them into small-group activities, she had her opportunity. No matter the subject, working together gave everyone a chance to learn between the lines.

> They just want to know, like, "Why do you wear the scarf?" or "Why do you guys have arranged marriages?" I don't feel weird about it—the more questions like that, the better. You can get ideas from students that never talk to each other. We're all people of color, so we should stand together.
> — HODA

At school, Shelby felt accepted by peers and teachers but also responsible to educate and advocate for other LGBTQ+ youth. She looked to neighborhood centers for support in that cause.

> There's barely any sexual education if you're not heterosexual, so people don't know how to keep safe. If they're trans, their insurances don't cover certain things. — SHELBY

And Wren, who identified as nonbinary, began to ask others to use *they/them/their* pronouns, instead of the pronouns assigning a gender that did not apply.

> In my early years of high school, I had a lot of internalized transphobia going on. I didn't really fit into any part of it, and I didn't know how to talk about that. — WREN

COLOR AND ITS CONFLICTS

Many youth of color said they daily confronted the differences between their own lives and the lives of others. Dylan, who was Black and transgender, felt doubly targeted by the police in his neighborhood. Even going back and forth to school, he felt anxious.

Finding Themselves When Binary Genders Don't Fit

In the "male/female" culture of high school, Wren Reeve came to realize their own nonbinary gender identity. Here they describe how that shift happened across four years and the issues that surfaced.

When people finally started talking about gender identity, it was a back-and-forth dialogue between a very binary set of terms, and I wasn't comfortable using any of them. Like, "Whoa, if I start talking about it they're going to 'other' me and I'm going to be even more outcast than I already am." I definitely felt a lot of fear.

But I knew how to conform to the ideals that people already had, so I tried to "pass" into certain groups. I was "othering" myself, in the school's hyper-binary setting. If I outed myself, I thought that I would be harassed and teased and bullied. And not only by other kids my age—I didn't know how adults in positions of authority would react. I never heard people on staff talk about being an ally. There was no visible representation of who I could go to for support—people with the proper training, in case you need someone who can talk to one of your teachers, or to other students in your class, or even to your parents. Teachers try their hardest, but if they've never had the training, how can they do that?

In certain classes, it makes more sense to bring gender identity up in context. For example, it would have been wonderful having someone to relate to in the history curriculum. Same with English language arts—writers throughout the ages were on the queer spectrum. In science, my teacher never mentioned a difference between perceived sex versus gender identity. Or the fact that intersex people existed at all. Or that some people felt differently about their bodies when they were very young than they did later. If I had gotten that before the sex talk, a lot more stuff would have made sense. If teachers talked about anatomy in scientific terms, versus very gendered terms, a lot of us would have felt more comfortable about our bodies and talking about them. – WREN

What if something happens? Do I really want to leave my house and risk it? I have to carry receipts now to prove where I went, because the police tried to say that I was somewhere else. I can't even promise myself that tomorrow's going to happen. – DYLAN

Others spoke of how peers from different backgrounds behaved in their presence. One of several Haitian siblings adopted by a couple in Idaho, Maelynne flinched at racist comments by fellow students in the first school she attended.

They called my brother Emmett Till—they thought it was funny, but it was dumb. And the teacher didn't do anything about it, which was frustrating. In our new place, it's not that racist, because there's Mexicans, you know. I've learned to deal with it. – MAELYNNE

Makiah, in Detroit, resented white peers who took liberties such as touching her Black hair.

Even if you feel like you're anti-racist, even though you feel like you're doing everything that you can, implicit bias and microaggressions still exist. Like, why do you want to touch my hair and nobody else's hair? That's a microaggression to me, that makes me feel uncomfortable. – MAKIAH

In Oakland, Kaliyah felt isolated in subtle ways.

It's hard to deal with another race if you've never been around it. Yes, a lot of people in our African American community have been around Caucasian people. But I've never had a Caucasian come to my house. You never have a real conversation, a bond. – KALIYAH

Her friend Shannon and his family also lived in a mostly Black neighborhood. Outside of school, he said, he did not interact in any meaningful way with whites.

It's nothing personal against them, it's just a weird situation. Like, if we need a favor or if we need someone to talk to, it's always an African

American person. One Caucasian couple recently moved in near us, and of course my mom welcomed them to the neighborhood and all that. But after that, not much interaction. – SHANNON

Their schoolmate Nyzja told of a Black friend whose family lived in prestigious Oakland Hills. When friends would gather at his house, she got to know white peers who lived nearby. But she felt uncomfortable reciprocating their invitations.

Seeing their big houses in the Hills was like going to Disneyland, just so amazing and extravagant. I was always afraid or embarrassed to invite them to where I'm living in East Oakland, me and my family cramped in a two-bedroom house. – NYZJA

In their social circles and their other communities in and out of school, these young people knew who they were—and who they appeared to be. Those identities and images had limits, many of them realized. They wanted to represent themselves in other ways.

Angel stood out as a popular athlete in his Bronx high school, for example. But he also sought out opportunities to change the stereotype of Black males. As a peer mentor for a nonprofit that supports students along their college paths, he found a way to make a difference.

There's a lot of stereotypes put on me, as a Black Afro-Latino individual. The image is not too pretty right now. But that doesn't stop me from being who I want to be. So I always carry myself with positivity. I try to show everyone who I really am. – ANGEL

Most students at Nyzja's Oakland high school were Black and Latinx, and she saw race and ethnicity fueling conflicts among them. When Latinx students casually used the offensive N-word, for example, Black students would retaliate with epithets like "wetback." Such tensions only got worse, Nyzja noticed, if teachers reacted differently to disruptive students.

We Are All Humans

Shortly before graduating from his Oakland, California, high school, Eric Nelson wrote this "speech for change" about the systemic racism he experienced in his community.

As a young Black male, I would like to say that we are not who the media makes us out to be. Yes, I'm Black. Yes, I'm tall. Yes, I go to public school and my family is low-income. But that does not mean we aren't good people. People should not be afraid of me.

Black people can't even walk into a store without employees following us around. But being Black doesn't automatically make me a thief. Is it the color of my skin that scares you? Me and you are both human. We both have muscles, and blood flowing through our veins. We breathe the same air. We do the same things day to day. We both can fight.

A few weeks ago, walking on the sidewalk in downtown Oakland, I saw a lady walking towards me. As she got closer and noticed me, she moved closer to the other side of the sidewalk, trying not to make eye contact. I find it ridiculous that just my being Black can make a person change how they walk near me. When unregulated stuff gets posted on social media, people learn to treat others like they are below them. But we are all humans. If we treated each other as equals, our world would be a better place. – ERIC

African American students are the main ones getting in trouble at this school. We'll be the ones to be told to quiet down, even though Latinos can be making a lot of noise across the classroom. When teachers start picking on certain people, they're turning us against each other. – NYZJA

Her schoolmate Kaliyah also worried about ongoing conflict among the school's Black female students.

We're always arguing over boys, or dark-skinned girls not liking girls with lighter skin. – KALIYAH

Yet when teachers increased their positive attention to a particular group, Nyzja observed, they also risked pushback.

When the book club started for African American girls, and when the teacher took some students to the Black Panther exhibit at the museum, other students had a problem with that. How do you make other people understand that maybe we really need this, to make our community stronger? – NYZJA

Their school typically gathers all students and staff for "community meetings" when important issues arise that involve everyone. Nyzja proposed using that structure to address the pervasive tension between Latinx and Black students.

We really need to talk about why we are having this conflict with each other. At the end of the day, we all have the same goal: trying to make it in life. – NYZJA

And Kaliyah suggested that the school provide additional support—perhaps in advisories or more informal groups—to help students respect their differences.

You can get other ideas from other people and understand where they're coming from—like what to do and what not to do. But it's difficult if there's not a space to do that and an authority helping us. – KALIYAH

Building a teaching staff that reflects the diversity of the student body—including race, ethnicity, and gender—can also draw in youth who otherwise feel disconnected from school. Nyzja had seen that happen, she said.

When we don't come from the same cultural background as our teachers, it's hard to build a relationship that can help us flourish in the community. But once we do that, then we want to come to that classroom and participate and learn. It's not about race; it's about having teachers who connect to kids, listen when you talk, and show they want you to succeed. They leave a mark on people's lives. – NYZJA

Laughing to Learn Together

At sixteen, Ben had been a minority white student in both of his New York City public schools. At the small dual-immersion K–8 school in his Dominican neighborhood, he felt ostracized by his classmates. But he finished eighth grade with fluent Spanish, which helped as he entered a high school of 1,600 diverse students of color—again, one of a handful of white students. Here he described some ways he found to belong.

> Just knowing Spanish makes me happy. You feel more in tune with people. I can know what they're saying in Spanish slang. I know what they're talking about, they know what I'm talking about, and we have this connection.

People often groaned at Ben's bad puns, and he soon realized that transgressive humor served as "a huge bridge builder" among the very different social groups of his high school.

> Like at lunch, a friend who's Black told me that most white people she knew wouldn't eat our cafeteria's awful food. Or if I raise my hand in class at a certain angle, they'll be, like, "Oh my gosh, he's a Nazi!"

Instead of bullying or posting rude comments online, his peers used such foolery to laugh at, and dispel, the political and social tensions that might divide them.

> We're just trying to calm down, in any way possible. The internet culture makes fun of everything, and we give that a physical outlet, where we can distribute our ideas and fears of how the world could come to be. And we're doing that in a community that's maybe more accepting than our families.

Outside of school, many youth of color are seizing opportunities that previous generations in their families never had. Entering environments where white privilege has held sway, they don't want to have to "educate" others on unacknowledged racism.

Angel, for example, took Saturday classes in science and technology through a Fordham University enrichment program. But college students on this Bronx campus look strikingly different from Angel and his classmates from nearby neighborhoods.

> With only four percent Black students on campus, I compare it to a bowl of cereal with white milk and little bits of cereal left in the bowl. We're the cereal floating around, and that's pretty much how it's going to be in a lot of places. – ANGEL

Angel and his neighborhood friends don't always want to play the trailblazer. Instead, they see themselves as beginning to normalize these boundary-spanning moments, which have the potential to change lives.

> You need to be comfortable with being uncomfortable. Meeting new people and learning about different cultures makes you more open-minded. You look at people for who they are, not what they are. I might be the only Black individual in the room, but I will make sure that I'm heard and I'm noticed. That's how I'll branch out and create a network—all over the world, if I can. – ANGEL

White students may also find both risks and rewards when they intentionally cross borders, hoping to learn. In rural Idaho, for example, Chloe joined a Latinx student group called Spanish Speakers Serving, although she had no Hispanic heritage. Her fellow students sometimes derided her for that, and even her teachers seemed baffled.

I try not to let that bother me, but sometimes it gets to me. It's a leadership program for your community and it doesn't matter what your ethnicity is. You're creating a bond you would probably never have. Nobody in the group has a problem with it, and that's where the opinions matter. – CHLOE

BORDER-CROSSING IN FAMILY LIFE

In their everyday lives outside school, many youth "cross borders" continually. They may be managing not only their own challenges but also the difficulties of the adults in their lives. They often care for their younger siblings, or their elders. Some hold down jobs after school and on the weekends, to supplement family income and pay their own expenses.

These adolescents also found that their developing beliefs often differed from those of their families. For Jennifer, whose parents came from Guatemala to Northern Virginia, religious and cultural issues proved the most delicate territory. She recognized that to belong and succeed in her environment she would have to move between communities, maintaining a careful balance.

At church, what the Bible says goes, but my political views differ. At school, not everyone has the same beliefs as I do. So I have to be very cautious about what I say and how I talk to people. – JENNIFER

Visiting relatives in Guatemala reminded her that other expectations prevailed in other cultures.

They don't ask if I'm in school, if I'm pursuing a degree, if I'm trying to do something with my life. They ask me, do I know how to cook? Do I know how to clean? I'm kind of tired of hearing that, because my priority is stepping out of those barriers. – JENNIFER

Other young people hoped to nudge their adult family members across the borders of contested social and political beliefs. Kaitlyn, in New York City, began

Looking Through Another's Lens

Marsela spoke here about both "school learning" and politics as explorations, in which people try to figure out what they think and where they belong.

Even if you're not an immigrant or the child of an immigrant, that feeling of "not belonging"—of being new—is something that we've all experienced. That's how I explain immigration to people who aren't immigrants. I'm really fortunate because my teachers openly talk to us about it. It's hard, but I try to believe in the system that is our government. I've always wanted to go into politics. My uncle in Albania has a dream of me becoming the president!

In tenth grade, for my global literature class, we did projects about how we want to change the world. I did it about immigration, the topic I'm most passionate about—we were reading the book *When I Was Puerto Rican,* by Esmeralda Santiago, and I related to it so much. I like literature, because it's something that we can interpret in our different ways. To me, it's a metaphor for how people believe in different things and react to things in different ways, even with politics.

For my project, I had to conduct interviews and get multiple opinions. It was very interesting to hear how someone's experiences very much shape how they feel and how they react to things. First, I interviewed five first-generation people, and their stories and opinions were very similar. So then I interviewed my art teacher; he had been a painter and then lost his job to an illegal immigrant. He hated and disrespected immigrants for taking his job away.

I asked him, "Then what happened? What job did you get?" And he said, "Oh, it all worked out for the better. I went back to college, I got an art degree, and now I'm teaching."

Even though life can get better, some people get stuck in a certain mentality. They have their own versions of life, based on how and where they've grown up, having different experiences, different educations. Everyone sees it in their own way, depending on the glasses they're looking through. – MARSELA

to try "active listening" instead of reacting to her mother's conservative points of view. At first she stayed away from political subjects, but one day she took a chance at respectful disagreement on an issue she cared about.

> My mom was defending a white woman in a TV news story, who had shot an unarmed Black teenager who came to her door looking for directions. I had to build this level of trust, by trying to listen to my mom. And then slowly we could get to the heart of the matter. – KAITLYN

At times, young people's conversations with family members enhanced and deepened what they learned through schoolwork. Athena's father, for example, had helped her widen her perspectives beyond life in Northern Virginia. Learning more about the larger world, she said, made her care about "more than our little space."

> My dad made my sister memorize all the nations in South America and then Africa, and now she's working on Europe. When you care about the rest of the world, I feel like it makes you a better person. – ATHENA

HOW TEACHERS CAN ACT AS BRIDGES

As these youth reached for their goals or crossed their borders, they could not always look to family for support. Yet teachers who knew them well had often opened doors to new discoveries. Students suggested the following ways to spark those generative interactions.

Engage with us outside class. When teachers facilitate advisory groups, sponsor clubs, and initiate hallway conversations, they help students—particularly children of immigrants—cross between various territories.

> The teachers and club sponsors here are great with supporting me to do what I'm passionate about. Our community service club has a peace committee, and we talk about topics and themes in our society or our homes. For example, "living in two worlds"—how it feels as a first-generation

student in America, with our parents not knowing what it's like, and getting accustomed to our public school system. – JENNIFER

At Shelby's school, advisory groups encourage students to stop acting as if "we are separate and therefore we are *always* separate," she said.

Even if you're not actively participating in advisory, you're in a human setting, not an academic setting. And it's created specifically so that very different people can interact and learn. It humanizes learning—making it more centered on how we are responding and reacting and what we're taking away from it. – SHELBY

Share your own stories. When teachers share their own experiences "crossing borders," those narratives have power, students said.

With one hundred or more students to look after, it would be hard to be personal with everybody. Just start with having an honest back-and-forth with us, stepping down from the teacher role and trying to know us. – CARSON

One teacher described how his family reversed traditional gender roles in their household routines, an encouraging model of flexibility. Another told honestly about her seven-year struggle to finish college. Especially if students' out-of-school environments signal tenuous or skeptical connections to school, an interesting story from a teacher can change a student's outlook.

My chemistry teacher would always tell us stories about herself—how she got her name, how she met her boyfriend—and somehow relate them to chemistry. A lot of teachers are probably scared of crossing the line between teacher and friend. – ATHENA

Give us new roles to try. Focused on their social concerns, youth may resist their teacher's pressure to engage more deeply in classroom activities. But they actually appreciate encouragement to cross new borders in their academic identities. Such challenges were preparing her for a wider range of opportunities, Rekik realized.

> They're helping us, by making us give presentations and switching our seats around. If teachers feel bad for kids who don't like it, they shouldn't back out so fast. When they make us go out of our comfort zones, we get more confident in ourselves. – REKIK

Rekik began to interact with peers she didn't know, even after sharing classes with them for years. She credited her economics teacher with nudging that process along.

> Afterward, I thought, "This is not that scary." Once you dip yourself in cold water, you're not going to get as cold anymore. – REKIK

Help us connect across differences. Kyle's teachers stayed alert to the tensions between students that might surface during class. Outside of class, they made time to bring them into conversation and forge connections across differences.

> By mediating a disagreement after class, a teacher can help students make things right. It helps them get over it, when they hear each other's side. – KYLE

Learning to build bridges in the school context may also influence how youth handle situations in other contexts. Kaitlyn learned to communicate better with her mother, for example, from the history teacher who welcomed controversy on tough topics.

> It's slowly helped me talk with my mom. First, I'm trying to have conversations without associating political institutions with our beliefs. It's important to have some sort of foundation: "On these things, we come together to a common idea. But we diverge here." – KAITLYN

Marsela, who worried about her parents' undocumented status, had also concluded that "party lines" did not help her navigate the territory ahead in an

Grouping Practices That Cross Borders

In a high school classroom, it's easy to make assumptions or judgments about others on the basis of differences (such as appearance or interests). But when teachers create an expectation that students will engage with others beyond their usual circle, it helps youth "cross borders" in community settings as well.

As they group students *intentionally* and *intelligently,* teachers deter youth from defaulting to their affinity groups—and lay the groundwork for everyday crossing of these borders.

Intentional grouping. A teacher assigns student pairs or small groups, rather than allowing students to choose their own workmates. The goal: peers connect with others who might interest them but whom they might not otherwise approach. Structures like "clock buddies" or "directional groups" provide simple ways to form groups.

Intelligent grouping. Taking intentional grouping up a level, a teacher assigns collaborators based on factors that either serve the activity or reflect some useful similarity (or difference) between students.

A survey at the start of the course helps to identify students' interests, hobbies, and experiences. And each time the teacher shares the rationale for assigning groups, it helps students appreciate the variety of strengths that lesser-known peers can contribute.

election year. Rather than defending a particular political stance, she was looking for ways to open the conversation with those who disagreed with her.

I feel like we're in a war with ourselves, always looking for what we can gain. We're arguing over things that involve all of us, but without trying to compromise about them. – MARSELA

When teachers take "crossing borders" as a learning objective, Athena noted, they help end that war.

> We're all humans, selfish by nature, caught up in ourselves. But in this modern society where we can be more comfortable, you don't have to compete with everyone for resources. There's enough for everyone. It's not evenly distributed, though, and that's the problem. We don't try to negotiate. By being selfish, we spark conflicts. – ATHENA

Coaching Students to Use "Accountable Talk"

Young people with ideas to share can benefit from practice in effective communication skills. One useful structure known as "accountable talk" builds the habits of supplying evidence for one's point, respecting the views of others, and participating in arguments in a diplomatic manner. To convey their reasoning, students learn to use certain sentence stems, such as "I believe ____ because ____" and "I agree with ____ because ____."

Teachers can integrate this approach into almost any discussion, and youth may also use it as they interact with their communities. Some useful contexts in which to practice accountable talk:

- Before introducing new material, to tap into prior knowledge
- After watching a film clip, to gauge a reaction
- During a read-aloud, to get students thinking about a complex question
- When debating a current event or an issue important to students
- Whenever students have to "prove" their thinking.

CHAPTER 4

Departing from a Single Story

"You can't put someone in a box where you think they belong."

The ever-shifting worlds in which adolescents now grow up have complicated the ways they see themselves and others. A single narrative—perhaps framed by heritage, color, class, gender, or sexuality—often cannot adequately describe the social identities that a young person may consider part of "who I am."

Miles, for example, resisted simplistic labels for his complicated genealogy, and connected it to what he wanted to learn.

> I have ancestors who came from Germany, ancestors who were in the
> Great Migration, mixed-race ancestors who were in Virginia and Georgia
> and Tennessee. The history of my community gets bigger as I learn about
> more places where people like me exist. I want to go to college mainly to
> learn Spanish and Portuguese, so I can talk to other mixed Latino people.
> — MILES

The stories that youth tell about themselves also intersect, overlap, contradict, shift, and refract—both in and out of school. They have grown accustomed to that fluidity. It shapes their interactions with each other—but their teachers often misinterpret it. Looking at a serial rule-breaker, teachers may not recognize a leader. Seeing a boy in a skirt, they may squirm to find a pronoun.

Yet when teachers acknowledge such elasticity, they can create opportunities to surface and to understand those shifting narratives. As youth and adults expand the ways in which they view each other, everybody learns.

Teachers often get their students wrong, Rekik observed. She thinks that her large Virginia high school often overlooks the possibilities—and the potential—of what's actually going on with youth.

> Maybe one kid in your class gets an F, or disturbs the class. That's not what they're all about. It could be they keep that persona in your class, but they're totally different when they get out. – REKIK

Young people notice when adults regard (and treat) them as inferiors—perhaps hostile, ignorant, lazy, deprived, or incompetent. When that happens at school, it can turn them permanently away from a subject, a teacher, or the school itself.

With an empathetic teacher, however, both sides can see things differently. A teacher can signal that it matters what the young person is experiencing. Youth can learn to express themselves in ways that convey their actual intent. Both parties can begin to consciously "depart from a single story" about the adolescent's choices.

> A "get to know you" quiz on the first day is one easy way to learn about students. Or just stop us after class and ask, "What are you trying to accomplish?" If they understand that, they'll see why I go about my work in the way I do and how I'm helping others. – LIAM

Andre began to develop a new perspective when a teacher spoke with him privately about his erratic behavior patterns in school. Their conversations inspired the young man to push against prevailing norms in a positive way.

> He's supportive. He tells me I'm a leader. If I want to do something that I shouldn't, he'll look at me and say, "Oh, you're better than that. *I* know you're better than that and *you* know you're better than that." Then I'll think, "Yeah, I am." – ANDRE

Seeing Beyond Stereotypes

As young people ask teachers to accept their differences, it's also important to recognize the (often accepted) use of labels and stereotypes in our culture. A courageous, explicit discussion—of their use and their effects—can prove useful in any classroom.

- What examples of labels or stereotypes can your students identify? Ask them to name ones they encounter in the various settings of their lives (school, home, extracurriculars, workplaces, places of worship, community gatherings, etc.).

- Which labels or stereotypes have they personally experienced (or seen a family member or friend experience)? Did those labels seem positive or negative?

- In what settings do people typically use such labels or stereotypes? Where do people tend to avoid using them?

- How, where, and when did these labels or stereotypes begin? How have they changed in recent times?

- What people do they harm? What people do they help?

Numerous organizations and resources offer free materials to help teachers and young people to see beyond stereotypes and labels. For example:

- On the website of Facing History and Ourselves (facinghistory.org), a lesson called "Identity and Labels" uses images, video, and readings to explore how the assumptions of others can influence our identities.

- The website of GLSEN (glsen.org) offers an hour-long lesson in which youth consider how self-identification can empower them and how being labeled without consent may damage them.

In everyday interactions with students, such teachers see past the negative behaviors of their students and instead convey a positive view of their potential. In the process, they may expand the ways in which youth view each other.

Athena, for example, had taken a fresh look at how she responded in conflicts with others.

Students Knowing Their Teachers, Teachers Knowing Their Students

Maelynne did not want teachers knowing much about her life outside school. She saw teachers' awareness of the details of her home and family experiences as an uncomfortable intrusion.

> I just want to get out of there. I feel like if I talk to teachers they'll treat me differently-ish—ask me questions and "how're *you* doing," and stuff. — MAELYNNE

Students felt otherwise if they had the chance to get to know their teachers better as people. In Kaitlyn's New York City high school, the faculty shared a large common work room, and students often dropped in to consult or ask questions. That broadened her perspective on how people learn from others, she said.

> In middle school, I never really saw the interaction between teachers. But here, I see teachers arguing. That's not a bad thing—it exposes us to different kinds of humans. That's important for schools: make sure you don't have all the same kind of person in your staff. And care not only if they're a good teacher, but if they're a good person. — KAITLYN

Both in schoolwork and in her personal life, Athena felt more inclined to take advice from teachers she knew better. Especially on high-stakes topics that involved risk, she said, it helps to hear an adult tell about a comparable experience.

> These stories matter, because they give you insight into the teacher as a person. I listen to their story for sure, and I definitely note in my head both the story and the message—instead of just, "Don't do this." — ATHENA

You need to look at yourself—how you're acting, what kind of vibes you're giving off. If you're yelling to get your message across, probably no one's going to listen. Evaluate yourself first and then the situation. – ATHENA

HOW DO YOU TEACH US?

In a world teeming with conflicting stories, teachers can help students find new perspectives—and youth can do the same for their teachers.

I don't like thinking, "Is this the answer the teacher is looking for, the one I'm allowed to give?" That just makes us wonder, "Is this the 'right' way?" – KYLE

Young people like Kyle are asking for a more reciprocal approach, in which everyone practices good listening in the interest of deeper learning. And when youth can see themselves in a topic they are studying, their motivation to learn also increases. Kaitlyn, for example, felt drawn in when her history teacher invited students to bring their own narratives into the curriculum.

Before that, I didn't care about U.S. history. Paul Revere, I'm not him! Our teacher allowed us to see ourselves in history in an organic way, not such a structured way. If you take the time to deeply unravel that whole yarn, you find something so beautiful and complex. – KAITLYN

Miles—who has an unusually complex family history—also entered compelling new territory when his teacher facilitated discussions about America's ethnic and racial identities.

That class was so grounding! It covered so many aspects of our history, in so many different tributaries, that I could actually see myself in it. There's so much that shakes up the viewpoint my mom instilled in me. What's important in your racial or ethnic identity? Is it even important at all? It's great when teachers pose questions that you can't answer— that you're not really *meant* to be able to answer. – MILES

Newsday Tuesday: A Conversation Protocol for Current Events

Any subject area can connect somehow with current events. This weekly fifteen-minute exercise helps students practice shared inquiry by exploring and evaluating diverse perspectives on the news. A teacher might model the process, then ask different students to select and present that week's article, video, or other media resource. The protocol "What? So what? Now what?" guides the small-group discussions that follow.

What? Help students share their understanding of the event.

- What have you read or heard? What have you seen?
- What questions do you have about what occurred?
- Where is the information coming from?
- What are the perspectives of those involved?

So what? Help students make sense of the event for themselves. (Acknowledge that they may have different interpretations.)

- What impact does this event have on you, personally? Within your broader communities? Throughout our country, or our world?
- What concerns does this event raise for you?
- What additional questions does this event raise for you?

Now what? Help students consider how to respond to this event. (Acknowledge that they may have different opinions.)

- What might you do as individuals or a group—either to share personal feelings about this event, or to take action?
- What next steps might you take?
- Share your group's answers with the larger group. (Goals: raise questions, develop shared understanding, explore impact, suggest actions.)

Useful resources: The *New York Times* "today's headlines" summary; "CNN 10" (daily news summaries for student discussion); Facing History and Ourselves (facinghistory.org); Teaching Tolerance (tolerance.org).

HOW DO YOU TEST US?

Just as young people may take different routes to conceptualizing academic material, they also can demonstrate their understanding in many ways. Students said they felt more invested in their work when their teachers allowed departures from the "single assessment" story.

By assigning diverse roles in group activities or projects, teachers often gain new perspectives on the capacities of their students. By encouraging study groups, or online apps, or community apprenticeships, they also empower young people to go after understanding, in whatever form works for them.

> Just finding different routes can help. I faced obstacles in biology class, and changing to different learning styles has helped me. – JENNIFER

Kyle wanted to use a more authentic voice in his academic papers.

> In science, there are a bunch of different ways to solve problems. And when you're writing an essay, people can still understand if you talk like you do at home. – KYLE

Athena and Maggie both doubted that standardized curriculum and assessments actually prepared them for the challenges of their future. "You can't test all animals by making them climb up the same tree," Athena said.

> My friend goes to a really tough high school, but they let you pick your classes and do clubs during school time. They have way more time after school, so you can explore a sport or a subject, instead of doing mindless homework for things you're not interested in. – ATHENA

> We should do a lot more project-based learning. It's a lot better than tests, because in the real world, you have to use your resources to accomplish your goals. – MAGGIE

These students did not feel confident that they could change the system. But they urged teachers to push boldly past the "single story."

> Instead of teaching to the test, teach us ways to use the life skills that get an A in life! How to pay our taxes, invest in stocks, raise a family, buy a house, cook a meal. Play the role of influencer. It's an even bigger role than a teacher. – LIAM

WE EACH HAVE MULTIPLE STORIES

Young people often hold their stories close in school, fearing that teachers or peers will pass judgment on them. Even those friends or adults who know what's really up may feel uncertain how to reach out to them.

> In class, you're seeing our surface—just one layer. Don't make someone into a "type" because of that! You can peel off and go deeper: it never ends. – REKIK

In rural Idaho, Maelynne grew up in a multiracial adoptive family with ten siblings; her adoptive parents have divorced. One of only five Black youth in the local high school, whose student population is half white and half Latinx, she spoke matter-of-factly in tenth grade about feeling left out.

> It was kind of a struggle when we had to do our family tree. I wasn't sure if I should put my real parents or my adopted ones. The other kids looked at me weirdly and asked a lot of questions. – MAELYNNE

Outside school, young people also feel vulnerable to stereotyping. Kaitlyn felt dismissed when others made assumptions based on superficial indicators.

> I connect more to my Mexican heritage than to my American nationality. People here don't see me as American—if I said, "I'm from Queens," they'd say, "No, where are you *really* from?" Some white guy selling eggs to my grandma in New Jersey actually complimented my English! But when you go to Mexico, it's "You're not Mexican, you're American." – KAITLYN

"I'm Going to Prove Them Wrong"

Angel, who played basketball for his Bronx high school, compared his moves on the court to what his teachers taught him about the tactics of effective debaters.

We say in basketball, "You've got to read the defense." You evaluate who you're playing against, their strengths, their weakness. Can they go left? Is their right hand dominant? You have to understand that everyone is different. Maybe my dominant hand is not his—I can use that to my advantage. You read the defense and transition it on offense when it's your turn to perform.

In a debate, you use the same thing—reading the defense and trying to transition it into offense. Let's say there's a class debate about slavery. I'm saying, "Slavery was a horrible system that dehumanized the minority group," and I have my facts to support it. The person opposing me is saying, "In the South this was their economic system. This is how their profits were made." On the defense, I would point out the weaknesses and strengths of that position and try to find a counterargument. If you sense you need a rebuttal, have that backup point as well. So let's say I notice that this person lacks background information. As an opponent, I will say, "Well, okay. Do you know how the whole slavery institution started in the South?" And then if that person doesn't know, I'll tackle that point.

Kids in my class love talking to each other. We've been known for debating among each other since freshman year. Sometimes the teacher says, "Enough! Let's go to the next topic." We agree to disagree. Like, "Listen, this is my position and this is why," and then another person will say, "Yo, I honestly don't agree with you, but this is why."

Even with the simplest topic, we dive into the information to point out every aspect. We touch all the bases, trying to highlight both sides of the argument. Our teachers teach us the skills. Instead of just saying, "Your claim is invalid and doesn't make sense," we can say something like, "I see where you're coming from, but this is why I disagree." If I agree with someone, I like to add on to the argument, like "This is why I agree with this point of view."

(continued)

"I'm Going to Prove Them Wrong" *(continued)*

Our teachers see how our mind flows, in debate. It's how we get exposed to different ideas, because everyone processes information differently. It's about analyzing information and also interpreting it, because everyone's interpretation is different. You have to listen and try to evaluate the whole situation. When it's your turn to perform, you have to be able to see their perspective and why they're coming from that. I might disagree to a certain extent, but I still want to voice my opinion. I can say, "Listen, this is why I feel this way. Maybe we can meet somewhere in the middle where we agree."

Not everything you see or hear is absolutely true. So you have to be open-minded. To an extent, you also have to be okay with taking certain jabs that people throw at you. You can even use that for your own advantage: "Okay. This person's putting me down. But I'm going to prove them wrong, in this way." If someone targets my ethnicity, I can easily discredit that with the great movements and culture we have as people of color. But you also need to know the strengths and weaknesses within your own culture. I guess that's why today's world is so divided, because everyone is so quick to make bad assumptions, due to what's portrayed in the media.

Kaynna, whose parents came from Ethiopia, wearied of trying to accommodate white people's fears and expectations. From childhood, she vividly recalled her mother's horrified reaction when she and a close white friend were shooting at cans with BB guns in the friend's backyard.

She was like, "If a cop strolled down her road, who would be in trouble? You, or her? Even if it's not your BB gun." Try all you want to make people open-minded, but there's nothing you can do. I'll always need to blend in, to not be myself. — KAYNNA

In a local restaurant with her parents, Kate reacted with fury as teenagers at a nearby table taunted them with anti-immigrant slurs. Her family's pacifist code kept her from speaking her mind, but Kate felt deep chagrin at holding back.

> I just kept glaring at those kids. I wanted to stand up and say, "Do you know anything about our story?" But my parents are not the type to deal with conflict, and they wouldn't let me. There was nothing I could do about it, and no one else was going to call them out. – KATE

Confronting the frustrations of their lives, these young people are everywhere calling on multiple strengths and understandings. In school, they hope their teachers will do the same.

SEEKING OUT OTHER STORIES

As they position themselves in their communities, youth are also discovering "who I am" and "who I want to be."

Jennifer, in grade twelve, was trying to move beyond the traditional role of the daughter of immigrants. She no longer wanted to translate the Latinx experience for others.

> Sometimes I have to walk away and forget about all the stereotypes. Hopefully I can educate the next person on why it's wrong to stereotype people. I would tell them the facts: you can't put someone in a box where you think they belong. – JENNIFER

Carson, an ambitious twelfth grader in a small town in Tennessee, expressed frustration with the limited expectations he perceived in his high school's culture.

> There's so much you can do—not just in high school, but after. Even if you may not think you like something new, don't be afraid to try. You never know what you might like. – CARSON

I Used to Think . . . but Now I Think

This simple protocol provides a way for anyone to reflect on how and why their thinking has changed on some issue. Equally useful for teachers and students, it helps consolidate new learning as people identify new understandings, opinions, and beliefs. At the same time, it develops reasoning skills and the ability to recognize relationships of cause and effect.

One can use this routine whenever one's initial thoughts, opinions, or beliefs might have changed, as a result of either instruction or experience. For example, people might use it after reading new information, watching a film, listening to a speaker, experiencing something new, having a class discussion, at the end of a unit of study.

1. **"I used to think . . ."** Before you answer, take a minute to reflect. Then, in just a few sentences, write down what you used to think about this topic. Start your sentences with, "I used to think . . ."

2. **"But now, I think . . ."** How have your ideas changed as a result of what you have just seen, read, or heard? In just a few sentences, write down what you now think about this topic. Start your sentences with, "But now, I think . . ."

3. **"And so I will . . ."** Given your new understanding, what can you commit to doing differently? This might involve an action, or a way of thinking, or a choice of how to work with other people. Start your sentences with, "And so, I will . . ."

4. **Debrief with others.** In a large group, small groups, or pairs, participants share, explain, and reflect on their shifts in thinking.

Adapted from Harvard Project Zero and protocols from the School Reform Initiative.

Many young people could describe times when they had learned meaningful lessons from others. Such experiences, they said, often took forms that

Finding the Right Question

People of all ages can find themselves in situations where they "don't know what to ask." The simple Question Formulation Technique, developed decades ago by the nonprofit Right Question Institute, helps both youth and adults to "depart from a single story." In the process, their thinking on any issue grows more complex, and they communicate their concerns more clearly. Participants in the group follow these steps:

- They brainstorm and formulate their own *questions* (rather than their *ideas* about an issue).

- They prioritize their top three questions, in order of importance. In the process, they learn to turn questions with one-word or "yes/no" answers into *open-ended* questions.

- They choose *one* question to focus on and brainstorm more questions about it.

- They design a plan of action to address that question.

Courtesy of the Right Question Institute, rightquestion.org

varied from routine classroom instruction. They didn't want their teachers to prescribe "what's right."

> Who makes up these rules? And who says we have to follow them? I'm just as intelligent as this person, maybe even more, so why should I follow what they think is correct? – KYNEDY

These students don't value ready-made answers. They want the tools and opportunities to solve their own problems, in both school and life. They appreciate learning how and where they can best find those resources. That will help them take the next steps—as they put their insights to use.

Help Youth Learn to Tell Their "Other Stories"

For young people to depart from a "single story," they have to recognize—and those around them must appreciate—that they have a voice. Teachers can empower youth to tell their "other stories"—those that differ from what they hear others say about them, or what they tell themselves. Some ways to encourage that shift:

- Recognize those who speak out. After a student has made a contribution in class, try telling her after class that you appreciate her courage. Or refer to her comment later in the discussion as "X's comment"—a small but affirming gesture.

- Support innovation and reward risks. Making something new both necessitates and perpetuates new thinking. Students find their voices quickly, once they don't fear taking risks.

- Let students disagree with you and encourage casual debate. Arguments not heard before can raise interest! Make sure students feel comfortable expressing theirs.

- Give second chances. Nothing feels worse than failing at your only chance to say something. When you see that happen in class, encourage students to keep trying.

- Let each student solve a unique problem. Don't make every problem a competition or give the whole class the same question. Students will feel personally connected to their own particular challenge.

- Invite each student to take some form of leadership. Whether or not they accept, keep asking throughout the year—it helps them realize it's not so scary.

- Personal missions. Get students thinking about their personal missions early on in the year, and every few months have them conduct "self check-ins."

Adapted from the website opencolleges.edu.au.

CHAPTER 5

Finding Our Strengths, Discovering a Purpose

"A teacher can provide the bigger picture we might not get at home."

I n the here and now, young people often don't view school as a place that recognizes their strengths. Many feel that teachers focus instead on their shortcomings—even as youth are developing important competencies at home, in the workplace, and in their communities.

Some see their schoolwork as disconnected from what they care about most. Those who diverge from societal or historical norms may feel invisible in the curriculum. And those with disappointing scores on college entrance exams have reason to doubt that a standardized test can judge their worth as thinkers and doers.

However, when teachers validated their strengths and identified a purpose that youth valued, these students found reasons to stretch farther.

> At my school, everyone on the staff wants you to prosper. They go above and beyond to help us, because we're all balancing academics with many other things. — KYNEDY

Such personal attention from school adults helps adolescents develop as whole people as well as scholars. A clear message comes across that both their lives and learning matter. As these youth discovered what they could do in the arena of school, they also found new strength and purpose elsewhere.

When teachers know their students well, academic connections come more easily. As Kynedy and her peers neared graduation at a Cleveland public school for the arts, their teachers had often seen them performing as poets, actors, and visual artists. Calling on those strengths in their classes gave students like Kynedy the motivation to engage in a range of subject areas.

> I daydream about different outcomes, about the butterfly effect. What if I get this job, travel here, meet these people? I know I'll end up doing something I enjoy, and if I can share that with others, I'll be happy. – KYNEDY

It can work the other way, however. In his tiny rural Indiana town, Liam aspired to colleges his peers didn't even discuss as options. Some of his teachers, too, casually dismissed his aspirations.

> You've dreamt of something and worked hard for it, and then your teacher says, "Why would you want to do that? I don't think you can." When you're learning from that person every day and they don't have confidence in you, it makes you take a step back. – LIAM

Youth like Liam don't want their teachers to ignore reality or steer them toward outrageous fantasies. They hope for the chance to develop their talents and interests into skills, and they need supportive coaching in that process.

As Rekik pointed out, teachers have an advantage—they can closely observe their students every day.

> Even though we don't like it, it helps when they tell us our strengths and weaknesses. One teacher saw me doing homework in his class for the next one. He told me, "You're a procrastinator—a bad one." – REKIK

When teachers, staff, and coaches give such candid feedback, they can influence adolescents' perspectives on both short-term and long-term goals. Carson,

Teach Us How to Make Our Case

Young people want their voices heard and their ideas to matter. They know that what passes as public discourse—in social media, in the news, and in classroom discussions—often lacks clarity, validity, and reason. And they wish they could make their case to others more effectively.

The Claim-Evidence-Reasoning (CER) model, often applied in science contexts, can also help youth explain their thinking in other settings. In a CER "explanation" someone starts with a question, then follows these three steps:

1. Make a **claim** that answers the question.

2. Offer **evidence** that relates to the claim.

3. Use a rule or principle to support their **reasoning.**

Young people might use the CER model to explore any topic that provokes controversy in a classroom or community. For example:

- Inequitable funding for girls' and boys' extracurriculars
- Dress codes that focus on young women and target particular groups or body types
- Course advising and counseling practices that track students into particular academic or vocational pathways.

Students might also use this protocol to consider their own academic trajectory. For example, they could draw explicit connections between their personal goals, their high school classes, and the actions and structures that support their success:

Claim: I will succeed in my personal goal of earning a college degree.

Evidence: In high school, I've had success when I made a connection to the teacher or the content.

Reasoning: If I pursue a college major that interests me, and if I can develop connections with my professors, I can earn a college degree.

for example, dreamed of a future in aerospace engineering but appreciated the realistic stance his teachers took. He had plenty of friends who were counting on an imagined future but hadn't begun to plan.

> You have to be your own person and also recognize that certain things are just not accomplishable. A teacher can provide the bigger picture we might not get at home. – CARSON

Still, these young people felt eager to grow into larger shoes. Rekik, for one, came to understand why teachers drew her past her comfort zone in class.

> I don't like it when they switch me from my friend's seat or force me to talk to other people. But it lets us know what's about to come in college and the outside world. You'll have to do different stuff with different people. – REKIK

OUR QUESTIONS AND IDEAS SHOULD MATTER

Maggie, a military daughter, had moved nine times before she entered grade eleven in a large high school near Washington, DC. Her familiarity with other countries had given her an appetite for knowing more about the world, but she felt excluded from the important conversations of adults. Eavesdropping on two people arguing about a Supreme Court confirmation hearing, she wished she could participate.

> They were saying things like, "Well, of course he would defend himself," and I wanted to interject myself. I'm only sixteen, but sometimes you need to say something. That's how you learn, that's how you gain experience: you listen and talk to people older than you. – MAGGIE

Barraged by media at every turn, many young people have trouble sorting out what they can believe. Rose, who has asthma, felt that tension when California wildfires made it intolerable to breathe her neighborhood's air.

Joining the Conversation

Natalie had gained a sense of agency from participating in an annual "Black Expo" at her Northern Virginia high school. But in her senior year, the school administration canceled the event after some white students argued for an explicitly racist protest they called a "Whiteout." Natalie went to her Englsh teacher, saying the decision was unfair.

> I couldn't believe it would be canceled because someone was afraid it would cause "chaos."

The school's solution: An "International Night" to be held after school. That timing greatly diminished the power and meaning of the event, Natalie said.

> I went to it and it was really nice, but not everyone went. Our school would have been more *whole* if it had happened during the school day. I told my English teacher how I felt, and she invited me to join a student group to help present alternatives to the administration.
> At first, I said, "I don't think so." I don't talk to those people. They're all white. They get good grades, and they have a voice. No one had ever put me in that situation, to speak to people in positions of power. But when we presented to the principal about how to build a stronger school community, I just let everything out.

I have to have a voice—to speak out about climate change, because future generations are going to be affected by whatever we do now. But social media feels overwhelming, with so many people everywhere starting to speak up. – ROSE

Her friend Hoda noted, however, that their school encouraged students to use such quandaries as a starting point for structured inquiry.

We have debates on topics like abortion and gun control and police brutality. We research an issue in a group activity, like a Socratic seminar. We have different ways to present our ideas, like an essay or a speech or an artifact. It's good practice. We're learning to have our ideas, listen to others, ask questions, and communicate with them in a respectful way. – HODA

The more personal the issue, the more learning it can generate. After Shelby came out at her school in New York, she sought out ways to educate peers on gender issues, a purpose that inspired her. "We come here for education and also to feel safe," she said.

I want to push for better sex education in schools—not only with the sexual part but also the consent part. We learn that you can say no to people, but how does the other person respond? That's very important, as is iden- tifying and preventing sexual abuse from a young age. – SHELBY

SCHOOL HELPS US CONSTRUCT NEW VISIONS

Youth from immigrant families often live with complicated tensions, as past, present, and future narratives compete for their allegiance. As their elders struggle to preserve their native cultures, the younger generation is adapting to new customs and expectations.

In many cases, these students told of educating their elders (or standing in for them) in the use of new technologies. Computerized processes used by schools, hospitals, and other administrative offices made the younger genera- tion crucial to the functioning of their families. For example, Jennifer described serving as an intermediary between her Spanish-speaking family and hospital staff, when her grandfather was dying of cancer.

Sometimes the older generation pushed against modernization. Hoda's religious Sunni parents came to Oakland from Yemen. While she strived at school toward college and a career, she knew her own independence would require breaking the family norms.

My father's very traditional, but he reminds us every day to focus on our education, that it will help us in the future. My parents expect us to suc-ceed—to support them and have a life with them. I love them—they worked hard to bring us where we are now. I want to give back, but I don't want to live with them forever. I want to go out and experience other things. – HODA

Yet many of these young people cared equally about the lands where they had roots. Raised in Northern Virginia, Rekik cherished a dream of someday working in Ethiopia.

When I grow up, I want to go back and make the wrong things right. I can't ignore my native country just because I came here and lived in luxury. I want to give something back. – REKIK

My Heritage, or My Future?

In grade eleven, Hoda struggled to reconcile her own dream of studying government at Stanford with her family's expectation that she would soon enter a marriage arranged by her father. She explained:

Traditional Arab men are always telling you that you're supposed to be in the kitchen. When you reach the age—after high school, sometimes it's seventeen, eighteen, nineteen, it depends—you're supposed to get married. My parents don't agree with my meeting someone in college. They want to choose someone where they have a connection with their family. My dad would not force us; he would give us a choice. He's like, "If you don't want to, you tell me. You stay at home and you can go to school. If someone comes in the future, they come." But we've changed. I tell my mother, "I'm going to go off to college." She's like, "Okay, you can get married, then go off with your husband."

What about freedom in other areas, too? I see what's going on in the government, and I want more people like me to have a voice. Now a lot of Arab people are stepping up, speaking out. Being Muslim, I'll have to work ten times harder—finding internships, applying for extra activities, keeping my grades up, going to office hours, seeing how I can improve.

When excluded from the governance of their schools, these students felt demeaned. They wanted a say in administrative decisions that affected them. At Rose's Oakland high school, for example, a popular Black administrator unexpectedly lost her job without explanation. Students should have played a part in that process, Rose declared.

> We're just not heard enough by the administration. Things happen behind closed doors, and they don't tell us the information because they think we'll overreact. But we care about these things just as much as they do, and it affects us a lot. – ROSE

At Emily's large suburban high school in Northern Virginia, a student texted her friends with racist comments about immigrants. Someone posted online screenshots of those texts, and then outraged students threatened the girl who

The "Secret Switch"	
If we need to learn . . .	*Don't switch back to . . .*
How to frame the right question	Defining our problem for us.
How to agree on norms of behavior	Handing out the rules for conduct.
How to come up with possible solutions	Making us choose from your selected options.
How to set parameters for action	Dictating the approved ways to take action.
How to assess the results of our work	Giving us the criteria for success.

had sent them. But when school officials disciplined only those who reacted, it caused even more unrest.

Emily wished that the principal had instead turned the crisis into a meaningful conversation. She took a certain pride in the pushback that her peers mounted.

> So many people were offended by the messages, and they went out of their way to show displeasure with the actions the school took. That revealed a lot more about our school community than the texter's racism showed. — EMILY

Young people recognize the subjective nature of their perspectives. But they want authentic practice in finding just solutions. They resent the "secret switch" that some school leaders use—first demanding adult-like choices, then flipping back to treating them like children.

STRENGTH AND PURPOSE OUTSIDE SCHOOL

Activities outside school also provide settings for youth to build competency and discover a purpose that galvanizes their learning. Teachers can support that process by passing along information about opportunities for their students.

Saskia volunteered with a national nonprofit initiative to educate youth voters. The experience gave her a driving desire to right the balance of national politics.

> Young people don't get heard much. The people currently controlling our government have way exceeded their time there. There's no diversification in terms of women, people of color. Old wealthy white males are dictating where health care goes, where gun control goes. That's really scary. — SASKIA

In his last two years of high school, Angel trained as a youth leader with a New York City nonprofit focusing on college access for low-income students. As he helped his Bronx schoolmates consider a range of postsecondary opportunities, he also gained new perspectives on his own options.

Every month we take students on three or four college trips: at least one city university, one state university, and one private college. We build early awareness, expose them to the campus atmosphere, give them information about schools they're interested in, and get them to talk with students there. – ANGEL

Many of his peers did not intend to go to college. Exploring their ideas for what they might do instead, Angel helped them start to map a realistic and satisfying path.

We help all students find a postsecondary option. "Listen, you're about to be done with high school," we say. "Everyone takes a different route in life, but we want to help you find the best way you can go about it." Otherwise, they just get their high school diploma and then don't know what to do. – ANGEL

Kaidyan, at fifteen, was working as a peer educator for a community health center in Brooklyn.

We talk to youth about how to have safe sex, prevention, how to protect yourself, how to get help if you need it. We gave out free condoms and information at the Pride Fest and we got people to sit down and talk to us. I enjoy it a lot—helping make sure that everybody is safe, just like I would want to be safe. – KAIDYAN

Marsela, who had come to the United States with her undocumented parents as a child, began volunteering in her neighborhood in third grade. At sixteen, she had priorities for how she could make a difference.

A big issue for me is equal opportunities in education. In the summer, I volunteer with City Parks and Recreation, helping teach little kids to play tennis. Children in privileged neighborhoods get so many opportunities. In what people call "bad neighborhoods," kids don't get the opportunities they want and deserve. – MARSELA

As a rising senior at her Detroit high school, Ama helped organize a city-wide student protest march for educational equality and racial injustice. In the Chalkbeat Detroit webinar that followed, she exhorted public officials to bring youth perspectives to the table.

> When you're running for office, make sure you're getting involved with youth. Invite youth leaders to the table to have those conversations, with the same respect that you would with any adult, making sure their voice is heard. And make sure your face is seen in our community. With social media, you can go on live with youth, get to know their expressions, teach them about what you're doing in the community, inspire youth in their community to run for office! – AMA

FORGING PERSONAL RELATIONSHIPS OF TRUST

Whatever interest draws them, young people can develop important social and emotional competencies in both school and after-school activities. Carson, a baseball player since childhood, said that team sports had given him "people skills" he would use whatever his future held.

> Even if it's a giant mix of people, you learn to work with them, to trust them, hold them accountable, let them know when there's certain things that need fixing. There's different ways to approach different people, but as long as you're honest with each other, you're never just standing alone. – CARSON

Liam, a high-achieving tenth grader in rural Indiana, often stayed after school to help out peers who felt unsure about an assignment.

> If I see a kid trying his best but struggling, I'll sit down and talk through the problems and help him accomplish his goal of getting a good grade. – LIAM

At home in Cleveland, Andre encouraged his younger siblings to build habits that would serve them well.

Activities for a "Purpose Gallery"

Students need practice in recognizing connections between their in-class activities, their current lives, and their future selves. Teachers can *tell* them about these connections, but it's much more effective to *ask* young people to identify these links. Even the act of asking adolescents for their opinions about such relationships helps them to consider the relevance of school and its lessons—and to trust their teachers and the topics they are addressing.

PART 1. "I DO"

As teacher, you model the activity first. Bring in a few photographs that represent connections between a topic you are teaching and your own life. Dare to share with your students a bit of a story about your world.

Examples: Science teachers planning a botany lesson might bring in a photo of their garden or share a favorite vegetarian dish with students. A teacher planning a history lesson involving military conflict might show a photo of a family member in uniform.

PART 2. "WE DO"

Next, you bring your students into the process. Provide a collection of photographs—some random and others linking to a class topic, the real world, or adolescents' lives. Ask students to choose an image that might connect to their lives, now or in their possible futures.

Example: From Google Images, choose a range of photos that evoke possible future careers (a woman in business attire, a hamburger, etc.) and supply a list of jobs predicted for coming decades. Students share their hopes for their own careers and tell why some jobs don't appeal to them. Explore together what next steps (including internships, training courses, or college) may lead them in the directions they want to go.

(continued)

Activities for a "Purpose Gallery" *(continued)*

PART 3. "YOU DO"

Next, students find and photograph a situation *inside* school that links to their current experiences or future hopes or plans. Then they find and photograph a context *outside* school representing such a connection. As a class activity or in a poster exhibition, students explain how their photos connect with academic subjects

Example: Considering what students have "pictured" regarding their futures, the teacher asks them about other elements of their current and future lives— their relationships, homes, communities, hobbies. Then they take pictures representing any of their goals: two in school and two outside of school. In each setting, the first photo should represent a "support" for a specific goal, and the second should represent an "impediment" to achieving that goal.

THE GALLERY

Finding photographs (for example, by searching Google Images) helps young people envision connections and goals. *Taking* photographs helps them see how to forge such connections and recognize the steps toward their goals. Displaying their images in a classroom gallery honors their ideas and validates their relevance to students' lives. As we make such connections to their present and their futures, we are building a collaborative culture of learning.

My fifteen-year-old brother doesn't want to go to school. I get him up like, "You have to go to school!" Small things like that lead to something better. If he's going to school every day, that's perfect attendance. – ANDRE

As students told of how they stretched themselves, the "small things" teachers did to support them played an important part. In the next chapter, young people think ahead to college and beyond, imagining ways that they might matter in their future.

Five Ways for Youth to Talk with Experts

Make an appointment for an interview. One or more students can contact an accomplished person to schedule a formal one-hour interview. If they record their interview on a smartphone, they can transcribe it and highlight what interested them most.

Invite several experts to a group dialogue. A class, club, or youth group can identify three or four experts from different fields to join them for a discussion about their paths to excellence. Plan for at least two hours and facilitate the discussion to balance adult and student voices. Refreshments can turn this into a special "power breakfast" or evening salon, but don't forget to take notes and reflect later on what the experts said.

Arrange student internships in the community. Schools with internship programs schedule regular weekly time for students to volunteer at community organizations. The best such programs gather students in a weekly "internship seminar" to debrief and reflect on their experiences. In this setting, one discussion might center on their close observations of accomplished adults in the workplace.

Ask an employer. Many young people hold down paying jobs after school. If they have coworkers or supervisors whose work they admire, they might request an appointment to ask questions about their training and practice.

Talk with family and friends. Parents, grandparents, relatives, and neighbors often have high levels of skill in various fields. Young people often find it easier to approach these familiar people for a recorded interview, and the adults involved are usually happy to oblige.

CHAPTER 6

How Will We Matter?

"What if I can only be me? Whatever that is."

Adolescents realize they are living in limbo—not quite adults, not quite kids. Although they want some of the rights that historically come with age, they don't always hanker for the responsibilities that accompany "adulthood."

But in these times, many young people believe that their lives depend on what they do in the immediate future. Like the generation that came of age in the 1960s, they are swept up in a rapid current of changing norms, which this time comes with social, political, economic, and climatic crises fearsome in their consequences. As this book goes to press, a pandemic of overwhelming proportions is destroying their hopes and plans for the years ahead. In the midst of its vicious physical toll, these youth know that its economic trauma could also leave them with lifelong scars.

Watching their world change and their country grow ever more divided, they are asking, "How will we matter?"

Teachers recognize those tensions when they know their students well. They witness both their ambitions and their anxieties—arising from factors that may include family expectations, work and career-related experiences, and community service. All those carry their different weights. But the habits and skills that teachers help youth build—particularly those that connect them across differences—matter at least as much in the world outside school.

Months before their Oakland high school graduation, Nyzja and Milan were thinking about how they might matter in college and afterward.

What Puts Us "At Risk"?
A group activity about our changing world

Educators use the term "at risk" to describe students who may fail or drop out of school. In these times, more young people consider themselves at risk in ways that reach beyond the classroom. If given the chance, they can speak to these issues—and help to address them. This group activity gets the conversation going.

Personal reflection and note-taking. Without identifying themselves, students write on separate small pieces of white paper (or white post-it notes) the issues that they think put them "at risk."

- As an individual
- In this classroom
- In this school
- In the local community
- In the nation
- In the world

A "snowball" discussion. With the room set up in a circle, ask students to crumple up their "risks" into "snowballs"—balls of paper—and toss them on the floor or set them on a table in the middle of the room. Each person gathers three random "snowballs" (avoiding their own) and takes a turn reading aloud the items collected.

Seeing solutions and making connections. Students and teacher discuss how to address each risk—individually, collectively, or through structural change (in school or in society). How might this class's curriculum connect to that risk?

Alternatives or extensions. If you deem your classroom culture sufficiently safe, students could collectively brainstorm these risks in small groups, then map them on a poster as a concentric circle (inner circle for their individual risks, the next circle for their classroom, and so on). You might use a "pair-share-square" strategy to discuss these issues. Each student chats with a partner, then each pair joins another, to further discuss these issues—identifying themes, considering solutions, and making connections to topics in the class.

I want to be a selfless, kind person who has an impact on people—they could talk to and rely on me. But I also want to be inspirational, like César Chávez or Martin Luther King, starting movements to fix what's wrong in the world. And I have personal goals for myself, too. – NYZJA

If you help someone, there's no better memory you can leave. It doesn't even have to be that huge. That's how a community gets rebuilt, and that's what school should teach. That makes me feel like we matter—learning how to do that for ourselves. – MILAN

Yet when these youth imagined community roles they could take beyond high school—and throughout their lives—many felt overlooked. Aside from family and friends, Alexza could not recall anyone in her rural Idaho community making clear that her participation would hold real value. "It sounds bad," she said, "but I don't think that's ever happened."

NEGOTIATING FAMILY EXPECTATIONS

The strengths young people see in themselves don't always match with the career paths and goals others want them to pursue. Whatever their family circumstances, youth often deal with the weight of heavy expectations as they grow up in a very different world.

Kynedy, a young Black poet, and Rekik, who wants to study psychology, knew that their families only want the best for them. Yet the dreams of family members weighed these students down, and they both pushed back.

Parents say, "You can be anything you want to be." But what if I can't be those things? What if I can only be me? Whatever that is. That's what I feel sometimes, and it makes me less optimistic. – KYNEDY

If you're Ethiopian, you're expected to go into medicine, engineering, or computers. I don't want to do any of those. I told my brothers I want to study psychology, and that led to a real fight in the house. They care about me, but they're fighting me about my own future, and that got me angry. – REKIK

Shelby, at fifteen, felt inspired to make documentary films. She regularly explored her Harlem neighborhood, using her phone to record interviews with people whose lives interested her. Her family expected her to go to college, and Shelby was already exploring that path—as well as where it could lead.

I want to shed light on issues like homelessness that people don't talk about. A teacher told me that New York City has more vacant buildings than homeless people! But my mother and grandmother have this picture of my future as a lawyer or something. I'm almost living in their lenses, and when I do things outside of those lenses they ask, "What are you doing?" – SHELBY

Her classmate Rob faced a similar clash with his Muslim parents, who had immigrated to the Bronx from Bangladesh when Rob was a child. They wanted him to study medicine or law, while Rob aimed to pursue a future in video or film production. But those conflicting priorities reflected many more.

I live in a culturally conservative family—every conversation goes to their wanting me to be more religious. For them, my hair being six inches long is bad! I am seeing things in a different way, so we're kind of colliding. Instead of staying home to do spiritual and academic stuff, I'm busy almost every day exploring. I want to know the options—to experience things for myself. – ROB

Gentrification in Hoda's Oakland neighborhood had influenced her decision, at seventeen, to continue living with her parents and support them as they aged.

This neighborhood is home, but it's changing—more people are moving out. When my dad first came here, rent was good. But now it's our whole salary. I don't feel like I can leave. – HODA

The Anxiety of "Success"

In their advisory group, Kaitlyn and her fellow students talked about their hopes, dreams, and priorities for the years after high school graduation. Reflecting on their conversation later, Kaitlyn said:

What seemed universal: "You have to do better than what you came from." We all feel this responsibility to the past. We want a safe boat, for the rest of our lives. One person broke down crying, saying they need to make more money in the future.

Other students say, "What if I don't have the money to support my dreams?" That's what's driven me to become this perfect, cookie-cutter student. All the steps I'm doing right now are preparing for "future Kaitlyn." She needs me to do the best and the most, so she won't look back and say, "I wish I'd done more."

But now I'm breaking down those ideas. I don't even want to use the word *successful!* I just want to be happy. I think I'm going to be just fine in five years. But I can also see myself, after college, really worried and nervous about what kind of job I'm going to get. It's kind of terrifying—what am I going to do if I don't have the money to support my family?

Other students set their sights on a future that would break new ground for their families. Marsela, who worried about her parents' immigration status, first learned the basics about finance in a two-day after-school workshop at a community nonprofit.

At school I joined a really cool finance and business club that meets Wednesdays during lunch. They teach us about stocks and investments, whether it's now or later, and how you can build up good credit. My ultimate goal is to be a financial advisor, also doing it pro bono for people who need advice but can't afford it. — MARSELA

Dylan was planning to leave California with his partner after high school, seeking a safer environment in which to complete his gender transition.

> My family is so strict on "Go straight to college. Finish. Get a good job." But I'm not going to go right to college without really having a good mental state. I want to take my time, find my true self, and then set my true goals: Go to college. Get the good job that I want. And live my life as myself. – DYLAN

CLOSE ENCOUNTERS WITH CAREERS

Many young people already spend much of their time earning money, out of necessity. They know the difference between "just a job" and a career, craft, or vocation. As they explore possibilities for their futures, their teachers can either help or hinder them.

In eleventh grade, Athena saw no connections between her schoolwork and a future that might interest her. She wished she could hone her thinking skills on real-world problems that opened new perspectives.

> School just teaches us to become workers. Sitting at desks, listening to one leader, you're discouraged from speaking. The teacher and others think your questions are annoying. You don't get clarification, and you lose interest. I was spending a lot of time just trying to have good grades, but I didn't know what I was going to do. – ATHENA

To get a better sense of which fields drew her interest, Athena turned to extracurriculars. Although her grades went down, she felt that she gained new purpose. In the debate club or through community service, she could see herself developing public-speaking skills and habits of organization that could apply to both school and the workplace.

In Oakland, Reevan continually sought out opportunities for low-income students that took place after school and in the summers. By grade eleven, she had lived on a Navajo reservation, backpacked in the Colorado wilderness, and taken an intensive STEM course on a college campus. As senior year approached, she contacted a nonprofit specializing in college access and support.

> My mom thinks that's it's going to be too much for me, with everything else. But I think it's helpful, because I'm learning time management!
> — REEVAN

Teachers who know their students well can often connect them with opportunities that support their passions. At fifteen, Kaidyan loved creating, singing, and producing his own music. When his advisory group took a field trip to a local university, he could picture himself in its recording studios, preparing for a profession.

> I think I would also be good at a career in health or counseling. But my first career priority is music, since that's one of my real talents. — KAIDYAN

If high school feels confining, students may check off its boxes and then check out. Jennifer, the daughter of immigrants and a highly accomplished student, figured out how to "do school" and won early admission to an elite college. But she developed a much stronger sense of agency after a teacher connected her with a GirlsUP club.

> After school we can find where we belong, with other people passionate about the same things. — JENNIFER

In her role as a student leader, Jennifer organized activities to break down social barriers among the very diverse students in her Northern Virginia high school. Her parents had come from Guatemala, and she hoped someday to start schools in countries where youth have limited access to education.

> My parents had to work when they were kids. They would walk barefoot to school, without the clothes and supplies they needed. — JENNIFER

Living in a Cleveland neighborhood where he often felt unsafe, Kyle chose instead to focus inward. For him, personal well-being mattered more than his career.

> We live in a capitalist society, and we just focus on the wrong things. Being yourself, that's the most important thing. Knowing yourself, and knowing love. – KYLE

BUILDING STRENGTH TO CHANGE THE WORLD

When thinking about their future, these young people tended to speak first about their families' expectations and their own hopes for interesting employment. Yet they also wanted to make a difference in their communities and in the larger world. As they looked around for ways to contribute, the avalanche of social media often left them paralyzed. They felt stymied by the deep divisions they faced at every turn.

They could already name their privileges and their vulnerabilities. They saw the sharp contrasts between schools for the advantaged elite and schools with mostly low-income students of color. During their formative years, the realities of gender identities had surfaced into plain view, often meeting with hostility.

Seeking to change such inequities, these young people often drew inspiration from the words and actions of others they admired. Kaynna, for example, had long wanted to "help the world." Now she saw other Black women working toward that goal.

> I like how our generation is very vocal, getting the word out about things that have been suppressed, like Black Lives Matter, gay pride. It's probably the best thing we are doing right now. Let people know, let them process it, and maybe they'll learn more about it. – KAYNNA

Milan and Rose appreciated adults who made space in class for them to engage with real-world tensions. Their history teacher, for example, brought in daily news reports of relevance to her Oakland students.

Leaving the Comfort Zone

Angel was in eleventh grade at his Bronx public high school when an internship with a nonprofit organization sparked his passion for journalism. He recalled his first assignment:

> They told us, "Look into a topic that you feel impacts your community." We learned what goes into interviewing someone and how to establish a bond so people can freely answer your questions. We practiced figuring out what points to highlight and what other small details would bring the piece alive.

With a friend, he interviewed shopkeepers for a story on gentrification in Harlem.

> Condominiums are going up, right next to the projects. We see different stores coming in, and stores from ten years ago aren't there now. We asked business owners, "Do you see your business here in five years?"

By grade twelve, Angel had gained hundreds of followers for his lively YouTube vlog, sharing his views on high school and beyond.

> I'm that person who likes to travel the city and record everything, so that experience inspired me to do vlogs, where I see new things and interact with new people. My personal slogan is, "You have to be comfortable with being uncomfortable."

I don't see the news every day, but I also don't want to be cut off from the world. Doing that every day, it's super important. She's making sure we're not oblivious, we understand what's going on. That's how a community gets rebuilt. — MILAN

It's not just us listening to her. I feel like she teaches us so we can teach her. She gets our opinions, and we hear what other students think. It keeps the cycle going, to spread the education. — ROSE

Not yet "out" to her family at fifteen, Roxy aspired to start an LGBTQ+ center in her New York neighborhood and to help educate others on their gender-related rights. As she read more about the history of her community, she began to imagine a scholarly future in that field.

> Studying queer history fascinates me, because they were persecuted throughout history. In the 1920s, when the Harlem Renaissance was happening, a lot of queer people were emerging, but it's really hard to find documentation of these events from before the 1960s. — ROXY

The college aspirations of many students reflected their unease about where they could belong. Kaliyah's older brother had attended a mostly white college, but he transferred because he felt disrespected there. He had recently earned his degree, at the same time that their mother earned hers.

Now, Kaliyah was considering a private university with a strong program in architecture. She aspired to start her own firm someday, specializing in residential architecture. Such a path would demand a lot, she realized, both academically and personally.

> A lot of stereotypes say that it's not normal for a Black female to have as much ambition as I have. I don't know if I would feel comfortable at a predominantly white college. But I just want to live my life by my goals. — KALIYAH

These students knew their family histories and often stepped warily toward their future. But many felt that new paths could open as they moved into life after high school. They already saw their generation "moving the needle" in matters relating to gender, race, and communication. Facing a perilous future, they were not abandoning their dreams.

Jeffrey, the son of Liberian immigrants, took a leadership role at his large suburban high school. In his senior year, he was balancing confidence and realism.

From day one, Black parents give their kids the talk: "You can't do some things that white kids can." I don't think we can change all of society. guess it's just something you live with. But if you know your own worth and you surround yourself with people who value you, that's going to resonate outward. There's no reason for you to stop trying to make the world more equal or solve its problems. — JEFFREY

TURNING TALK INTO ACTION

With a mix of dread and pessimism, these students recognized that existential threats loom over their generation's life span. Many of them—particularly young males of color—had grown up with the threat of violence from the police and other authorities charged with protecting them.

"We're not all sheep," said Jordan, a Black student from Minnesota whose anger spilled over in words through his hip-hop stanzas:

We need to take action . . . All this talking is gonna get you killed 'round here, you know? — JORDAN

Other students felt betrayed by the government's reluctance to regulate gun ownership despite recurring massacres in schools and other community settings. After seventeen people died from gunfire at a high school in Parkland, Florida, Natalie and her peers asked the administration of their Virginia school to take preventive action.

We say these things to them, but nothing changes. They say they're going to do something, but it looks like they don't care. — NATALIE

Roxy worried about the impact of climate change on her home, her community, and her life. "I've seen some maps where New York City is underwater, along with a bunch of other coastal cities," she said. But that issue seemed more distant than the other problems she confronted day to day.

I worry about the hate crime rate going up, especially towards LGBTQ people. And accessibility rights—almost no subway stations in New York City have a way for disabled people to get on the train! Voting gives you the power to try and change that. But I worry about gerrymandering—my district might get rezoned, and that's not a good thing. – ROXY

In her AP government class, Rose chose to explore the question "Are elections free and fair?" Volunteering in Oakland as a poll worker, she found some answers.

Polls in low-income areas are really low on staff. There's no machines, so lines are longer. The longer people wait, the more discouraged they are to go vote. – ROSE

"It starts with just having the conversation," said Saskia, who volunteered with a nonprofit initiative that emphasizes civic education and voter registration for youth.

In the last election, a lot of people didn't vote because they didn't know how, or where to go. Many high school students don't even know how to fill out a ballot. We do social media campaigns with friends who are going to be eighteen, telling them where they can register to vote. – SASKIA

As Natalie struggled, in her fifth year of high school, to overcome the many obstacles to her diploma, she came to recognize the possibilities that lay in herself and her communities.

Sometimes I can look at someone and see how they are, in just one second. They might act like they're so bad and they don't care, but I'm like, "Wow, I know this is a really good kid." – NATALIE

She paused and then came to her conclusion: "That's what the best teachers do."

Part II | What Youth Can Do

Overview: Youth Can Make Change

Briefing 1. Youth Action on Climate Change

Briefing 2. Youth Action on Violence in Their Communities

Briefing 3. Youth Action on Voter Engagement

Briefing 4. Youth Action on Immigration

Briefing 5. Youth Action on Gender Identities

Youth Can Make Change

L istening to the young people in the previous six chapters may leave educators with both new insights and new worries. They hear the tensions that students bring to the classroom, often darkening their vision of the future. But what can teachers really do to address the intractable challenges of our time: climate change, violence in our schools and streets, electoral inequities, immigration, gender identity, and the forces of color and money that saturate all those issues?

Any opportunity for youth to use their minds, of course, will sharpen their ability to address contemporary dilemmas. History can shed light on present crises; other languages can lead to cross-cultural dialogue; mathematics can model problems and solutions; science can strengthen critical thinking; art can express emotions without words. Good teachers know this and often link subject-area curriculum with the issues that most engage their students.

Yet the fires are spreading quickly as today's adolescents grow up. They need practice in addressing matters of urgent importance to their communities. When teachers support their exploratory steps, new possibilities emerge. Young people begin to act in the public sphere or deepen the actions they have already started. Educators contribute how they best can—in the classroom, in extracurricular contexts, and as resourceful allies in organized action outside school.

This part of our book features five change areas where that process is taking place. Youth speak from their own experience in each area; educators and youth development organizations contribute proactive examples. As those perspectives connect and combine, they enrich and extend the high school curriculum.

10 Questions to Guide Civic Action Projects		
QUESTION	**STEP**	**VALUES**
1. Why does it matter to me?	Step 1: The Power of Narratives	Equity
2. How much should I share?		Self-Protection
3. How do I make it about more than myself?	Step 2: From "I" to "We": Equitable Issue Identification	Equity
4. Where do we start?		Efficacy
5. How can we make it easy and engaging for others to join in?		Efficacy
6. How do we get wisdom from crowds?	Step 3: Investigation and Researchs	Equity, Self-Protection
7. How do we handle the downside of crowds?		Equity, Self-Protection
8. Are we pursuing voice or influence or both?	Step 4: Voice or Influence Choosing an Action Strategy	Efficacy
9. How do we get from voice to change?	Step 5: Voice *and* Influence: Implementing a Plan	Efficacy
10. How can we find allies?		
Step 6: Reflection and Documentation: Review of Answers for All Questions		

Source: The MacArthur Research Network on Youth and Participatory Politics, Harvard University Democratic Knowledge Project, and Facing History and Ourselves.

Whatever societal issues youth and educators take up, they can find important guidance in a superb framework for civic action developed in a decade-long partnership of the MacArthur Foundation's Research Network on Youth and Participatory Politics, Harvard University's Democratic Knowledge Project, and the nonprofit Facing History and Ourselves. Its ten clarifying questions prioritize equity, self-protection, and effectiveness as young people participate in democratic action. (See previous page.)

For example, Facing History's curricular units, which probe contemporary and historical issues, use those questions to help youth navigate the raw challenges they face in real time. Students start with their own personal narrative and their stake in the matter at hand. Then they make it about others, too, whose experiences and stakes may differ. They decide where to start and how to sidestep predictable snags. In the end, they decide the priority for their action. Raising their voices to influence public opinion? Affecting policies made in the halls of power? Perhaps it's both—and that also can shape a strategy for change.

The themes explored in Part 1 of this volume emphasize the social and emotional development of adolescents living and learning in an era marked by unprecedented changes. As students described their challenges and needs, some viewed their teachers as important "influencers" in their lives. Others, like Rekik, saw high school as "just a small part of a big world where a lot of bad things are going on." As they looked for ways to build their strengths and find their purpose in that world, many felt as Carson did: "A teacher can provide the bigger picture we might not get at home."

At the same time, youth themselves can provide a crucial infusion of urgency and energy in confronting this era's challenges. Their modes of communication vault over barriers to access; they galvanize their peers with ephemeral "flash activism." They break the rules, asserting that the future of their planet outweighs

Friday afternoon in school. In the following pages, Part 2 presents examples of how youth around the country, with support from adult allies, are claiming their place in the bigger picture. Organized around high-profile issues that youth are confronting, it provides a sampling of entry points and materials that might help young people get involved in local, state, or even national arenas.

"Start where students are"—the most important maxim of teaching—provides a touchstone for how best to use these resources. We know that youth will take it from there.

I Took It on Myself

Born and raised in East Oakland, California, Ivan Garcia by ninth grade was working on several fronts to support causes that mattered to his generation. This excerpt has been adapted, with permission, from Sam Piha's March 6, 2019, interview of Ivan Garcia for the blog *Learning in Afterschool and Summer* (learninginafterschool.org).

> Following the 2016 presidential election, my eighth-grade classmates and I felt that we needed to speak up and share our opinions. I took it upon myself to create a class video of our opinions, fears, and hopes, titled "Dear Mr. Trump." By early 2019, that video had over four thousand views, connecting with many young people who felt as though their voices weren't being heard.
>
> That led to my serving on the Oakland Youth Commission, which advises the city council and mayor on issues affecting youth, including the March for Our Lives Oakland rally against gun violence. Now I am an intern in the mayor's office, learning the inner workings of city hall and hearing from many constituents.
>
> I'm also on the youth advisory board for Youth Tech Health (YTH), a nonprofit that uses technology to advance the mental and sexual health of youth all around the world, especially developing nations. Most recently, I helped with a text campaign they have going on in Honduras currently, which tackles the issue of teen dating violence. We do lots of outreach to groups, including in the LGBTQ+ community. Also, I act as a youth ambassador for Litterati, an app that uses crowdsourcing to document environmental degradation worldwide.
>
> Youth activism equips us with essential skills: networking, organizing, public speaking, even drafting policy. At the same time, we need

the freedom to try our own unique ways of expression. Don't limit our perspectives—instead, provide safe spaces where we can feel free to be ourselves. Adult allies should support the work of young people but not take over and determine the way that work should be done. Students themselves should do that. To motivate us, bring people in who are doing this work as an example. It's one way that we can see what's possible, as we think about more than just ourselves.

Most recently, youth have been invested in gun violence, given the many incidents that have rocked our nation. Following Parkland, many young people created groups and organizations that are still doing meaningful work in their communities. Other areas of interest for youth, I think, include criminal justice reform, sexual assault and harassment, and education (especially in places where schools are underfunded and under-resourced).

Creating an environment that encourages truth and honesty can go a long way for young people who want to be active in their communities. Lately, I've taken a step back from some of my previous work, to engage in deep discussions with many of my peers. It's been humbling to be in spaces with people my age, discussing things that matter to us. I hope to work on a project that helps all young people to find what inspires them, to love themselves for who they are, and to fight for a better tomorrow.

Conversations Build Student Agency

Taking seriously the concerns, reflections, and actions of youth both shows respect and encourages them to act as civic agents, writes Laura Tavares in a blog for Facing History and Ourselves.[1] Whether teachers endorse their opinions or not, they can offer important support for young people's right to expression. If students share their intention to join walkouts or other protests, a supportive open-ended conversation might include questions, such as those that follow, about the range of ways to make a difference.

- Why are you interested in joining the walkout?

- What do you know about what's happening, and what do you have questions about?

- How are you educating yourself and others?

- Where can you find friends and allies?

- What might be some consequences of your participation?

- What impact are you hoping to have?

- Beyond the walkout, what are other ways you can stay engaged to push for the change you seek?

Can Schools Punish Students for Protests?

Can schools discipline students for speaking out? It depends on when, where, and how youth express themselves, according to the American Civil Liberties Union (ACLU).[2] Some examples to share with activist youth follow.

Planning a walkout: Your school can discipline you for missing class, just like they always can. But it can't punish you more harshly for a protest walkout than it would if you were missing class for another reason. Before your walkout, know the potential consequences. Find out what policies govern discipline for student absences—in your state, your school district, and your particular school.

Protests during school: Schools cannot legally impose punishment on some forms of student protest. For example, you cannot be punished for speaking out during school hours, unless your speech disrupts the functioning of the school. What qualifies as "disruptive" will vary by context, but courts have typically held that students have the right to wear expressive clothing if it doesn't target fellow students or disrupt class. The Supreme Court has ruled that students are protected by their constitutional rights when they wear political armbands or refuse to salute the flag.

Protests after school: Outside school, students enjoy essentially the same rights to protest and speak out as anyone else. Therefore, youth are likely to be most protected if they organize, protest, and advocate off campus and outside of school hours. Some schools have attempted to extend their power to punish students for off-campus and online expression. While courts have differed on the constitutionality of such punishments, the ACLU has challenged such overreach.

A CIVICS TOOLKIT

Wanting to Matter, but How?

Overwhelmed by issues, yet hoping to contribute, youth need support as they explore their possible participation, whether face-to-face or online. Drawing on recent work by the MacArthur Research Network on Youth and Participatory Politics, a team from the University of California created a Digital Civics Toolkit, a substantial curriculum resource to help youth develop into informed, engaged, and effective participants in their communities.[3]

Its five modules start with exploratory questions and connections, then guide youth through activities, critical thinking, and dialogue in an area of their interest. As they decide how and where to express their ideas, and what actions they will take, they are growing their capacity to make change in their world. The following questions form the backbone of that five-part process.

Explore

Who do I see as my face-to-face and online communities?

What civic issues do I hear people in my community talking about most?

What civic issue am I curious about that I'd like to understand better and get involved in?

Investigate

Why is credibility important? How can I judge the credibility of civic information online?

How can I reflect on my biases when investigating civic issues?

How do I understand and analyze visual forms of civic information online?

How do I investigate a topic and present what I have learned?

Dialogue

What are the opportunities and challenges of in-person vs. online dialogue about civic issues?

What do "good" and "not so good" online discussions of civic issues look like?

How can we make good online dialogue about civic issues happen?

Voice

How do I find my story and express it in ways that are civically meaningful?

What do I choose to share publicly, and what do I keep to myself?

As I express myself, how will my message spread?

How do I manage the "digital afterlife" of my voice?

Action

What can we learn from social change efforts from the past?

What does it mean to take action around social issues in the digital age?

Is online activism "slacktivism" or just another way to take action? What are the risks?

How do we determine a course of action using social media?

Editorial Cartoons as "Artivism"

"Artivism" has caught the imagination of young changemakers who express political opinions in popular art. A curriculum from the nonprofit Teaching Tolerance (tolerance.org) builds on that interest, using editorial cartoons that address social justice issues, now and in the past. Its mix of visual art, language arts, and social studies culminates with students creating their own editorial cartoons on an issue of their choice. Some examples:

Racial profiling: how a cartoon uses irony.

Censorship: how images combine to make a point in an editorial cartoon.

Poverty and environmental justice: how a cartoon uses satire.

Gay rights: how a cartoon uses idioms and puns.

Equal opportunity: using familiar adages in new ways to make a point.

Immigration debates: in a historical context, how a cartoon made a political statement using irony and caricature.

Language diversity: the importance of context in decoding an editorial cartoon.

Bullying: how cartoon artists use images to represent an idea.

Gender discrimination: how cartoons use words and images to make a political statement.

Racism: how artists use titles to bring context to editorial cartoons.

Hate: how editorial cartoons use dialogue to question hatred between groups.

Eight Resolutions for Young Changemakers

The nonprofits Next Generation Politics (nextgenpolitics.org) and YVote (yvote. org) partner in coaching youth to lead civic-oriented events and get out the vote. Both those activities take hard work and practice, says their director, Sanda Balaban, who offers these "resolutions" to ward off burnout in young activists.

Resolution 1. Burnout. Is. Real. Nourish yourself, take breaks when needed, and have compassion for yourself, too. If you won't rest until the world's problems are resolved, you're on a one-way street to burnout!

Resolution 2. Don't make politics your identity. Whatever your beliefs, enjoy time with those with different beliefs—and maybe even learn from them

Resolution 3. Remember what fuels your passion. There's a reason you're sacrificing your sleep, schoolwork, and sanity. Look toward your North Star and let its light reenergize you.

Resolution 4. Stay truly informed. In this decade, we want to counteract gross generalization and the zealous spread of misinformation!

Resolution 5. Stay calm and rational. When you get angry, people react to your attitude instead of the point you're trying to make. Staying calm shows true strength.

Resolution 6. Be open to new information. The things we *resist* the most are often the areas where we can *learn* the most.

Resolution 7. Have more fun while doing good! If it's not fun, you won't keep doing it, so what's the point?!

Resolution 8. Start *now*! Goals and resolutions mean nothing if we do nothing. So stop falling into the rabbit hole of Instagram, and get started!

Youth Action on Climate Change

A worldwide youth protest against climate change ignited in 2018, when Greta Thunberg, at age fifteen, began skipping school in Stockholm every Friday to stand alone outside the Swedish parliament with a handmade poster reading "School strike for climate." Inspired by her example, U.S. students have joined those from other countries in weekly "Fridays for Future" strikes, pressuring lawmakers to stem the environmental catastrophe that will radically affect their generation.

By 2019, the Sunrise Movement, a youth-led climate change advocacy group, had helped draft the "Green New Deal" proposal: a national transition to renewable energy, expanded public transportation, and an economic plan to drive job growth. By Earth Day 2020, major youth lobbying organizations such as the U.S. Youth Climate Strike coalition had organized three days of strikes, rallies, protests, and teach-ins. Other youth-driven efforts were also having important impacts on policy, both in local contexts and on the national stage.

This section sets out actionable information for both youth and adult allies who are looking for ways to make a difference in their schools and their communities. "You can start small and get bigger," said Adam Neville, a high school student who coordinates New York City's chapter of Extinction Rebellion Youth, one of many climate-centered youth organizations across the United States.

Such groups can amplify their voices through the national Alliance for Climate Education (ACE), a forum where youth around the country share on video their stories of climate activism. Educators may also draw freely on ACE's multimedia "Our Climate Our Future" video series, a lively mix of conversation, information, and animation that explains the science behind climate-related crises as well as the technologies that address them.

At the United Nations, the Secretary-General's Envoy on Youth serves as a global advocate for addressing the needs and rights of young people and offers abundant resources on climate change. Eighty percent of the world's young people live in developing countries, where climate crises pose major threats to their health and socioeconomic stability. The U.N.'s program of small grants has helped nearly half a million youth worldwide to take climate-related action.

Success in such endeavors may depend on youth developing the skills to influence lawmakers, big business, and others whose decisions affect climate change. This section includes suggestions for how this might happen. And the learning goes both ways. Teachers can help students to write cogent letters and speak powerfully in public, just as youth can demonstrate how video, social media, and slogans can resonate across generations. Boycotts, marches, and other purposeful demonstrations require careful planning, organization, collaboration, and communication—all basic skills in any school's curriculum. For everyone living in the years ahead, the "exam" will happen all too soon.

Not Resigned to the Apocalypse

In his senior year in high school, Adam Neville, seventeen, coordinated the New York City chapter of Extinction Rebellion Youth. In our interview he described how the group works, and why it matters to the climate crisis.

Climate activism is strikingly youth-led. In New York, we have Extinction Rebellion, Fridays for Future, Zero Hour, Sunrise Movement, and many other youth climate groups. We're all aiming to reach the public, the press, and politicians, so together the New York groups formed a Climate Strike Coalition. This fall, we organized two major climate-strike street demonstrations.

Those organizations often have different strategies. For example, Fridays for Future strikes every Friday, with youth around the world leaving class to protest government inaction. Its New York chapter strikes in front of the United Nations. Our group, Extinction Rebellion Youth NYC, holds biweekly Sunday meetings. Extinction Rebellion is also an international group, but in the United States we have four demands.

First, we want the government and the media to tell the truth about the climate crisis. Second, we want the government to act now and go carbon-neutral by 2025. Third, we want a citizens' assembly to make public the very different impacts that the climate crisis has on people with diverse backgrounds and circumstances. Fourth, we want an equitable transition away from fossil fuels and pollutants. Not every person is approaching this crisis from the same place. Some people have jobs that ultimately contribute to pollution, but they need to make ends meet. It's about giving what we can.

That last point matters a lot to our New York chapter. When we demonstrate in the streets, some of us are willing to get arrested. We had lawyers come to one of our meetings, and we studied the way civil disobedience law works and possible interactions between the police and protesters. Our recent demonstration in Herald Square was a meditation in the streets, blocking traffic so cars couldn't move through. The police gave us a warning to clear the street, and those who didn't want to get arrested cleared out. Not every person who's participating in this movement can give the same thing. All four members of our group who were willing to be arrested were white, from fairly privileged backgrounds; three of them were fifteen, and one was seventeen. They stayed to make a point, and they ended up getting out of police custody within roughly six hours.

You hear a lot about "climate anxiety." It's very real, especially because Generation Z has a taste for nihilistic humor, which I love. But the fight against climate change is not lost. By no means are we resigned to the apocalypse. The solution is out there: everyone working together. Our lives are not over. At the same time, that anxiety—the feeling that "I deserve a future"—is what gets so many of us involved.

Everyone can do something about the climate crisis. You can start with your personal life: How much trash you're using; whether you can save paper by submitting that assignment digitally. Maybe eat less meat or try a vegetarian meal. Switch to reusable eating utensils and bring your lunch in containers you can use again. Find out if your school actually recycles—you might be surprised where those recycling bins end up. Small things like that contribute, and they're all really valuable.

You can also talk with teachers about incorporating climate-related material into their classes. Can our science project focus on climate issues? Can we write an English essay on this book about the climate crisis? Can we analyze climate-related statistics in math class? Lots of schools are looking for practical applications of concepts in the curriculum. No subject exists in a vacuum; they connect to one another. And the classroom connects to the community—it relates to every individual's status as a global citizen in our era. It can function as a conduit to social action. I don't see why that can't be a national standard.

Protest is the face of the movement right now. You learn to have conversations with power. You can start small and get bigger. Talk with your principal: can you organize a school club? Reach out to the climate movement in your city, state, or region, for information and action plans. Email or mail a letter to your local representative. Talk to local stakeholders and elected officials who have a say in what goes on in your city.

When you strike, it's big. There's a cool picture of Greta Thunberg at one of her very first strikes, sitting against the wall with one sign. Fridays for Future suggests you do that every Friday, to connect your action with so many other youth around the world. With a lot of legwork from that group, our coalition secured an amnesty agreement with the Department of Education about civil disobedience by students. Even if you're striking alone, you make the point visible: "I can't do school today because I'm so concerned about this. I need my elected officials to do something."

Pushing for Climate Justice

"Our diplomas may say Class of 2020—but marked in history, we are the Class of Zero." In graduation speeches, many students now are "taking the pledge" to vote for candidates committed to zero emissions from fossil fuels. The 300,000-strong youth action network that launched that idea is part of the Alliance for Climate Education (ACE), which since 2009 has educated 3.5 million young people to take action on the climate crisis.

The ACE website (acespace.org) offers a host of free, lively multimedia videos that draw youth into climate science. Interviews with young activists on its series "Our Climate Our Future" show how to take meaningful action. The organization sponsors a year-long "action fellowship" that has trained four thousand youth in climate advocacy.

Not least, countless graduation audiences by now have heard "The Speech." Created by Class of 0000—a youth-led movement to build a coalition of first-time voters prioritizing climate action (classof0000.com)—it goes like this:

> Today, we celebrate our achievements from the last four years. But I want to focus on what we need to achieve in the next eleven. That's how long climate scientists have given us: eleven years to avoid catastrophic climate change. It's already damaging our homes, our health, our safety, and our happiness. We won't let it take our futures, too. Our diplomas may say "Class of 2020," but marked in history, we are the "Class of Zero." Zero emissions. Zero excuses. Zero time to waste. Across the country, our class stands 7.5 million strong. And in unity, we're giving 2020 political candidates a choice: Have a plan to get to zero emissions, or get zero of our votes. Together, we have the power to solve the climate crisis. Every student. Every parent. Every teacher. Every leader. The future is in our hands.

Climate Fact or Fiction

This quiz (and others like it), adapted from an activity developed by Connect4 Climate and Earth Day Network (earthday.org), assesses knowledge about climate change. Directions: First, **respond** to all the questions. Next, discuss your answers with peers and teacher and decide if you want to **reconsider** your responses. Then use your most reliable resources to **research** the best answer to each question.

1. Present-day accelerated climate change is caused by:

   a. Solar flares

   b. The earth's rotation around the sun

   c. Volcanos

   d. Human-produced greenhouse gas emissions

2. The U.N. Paris Climate Change agreement aims to:

   a. Set a goal of limiting the global temperature increase to less than 2°C (3.6°F)

   b. Identify the countries that pollute the most

   c. Create more jobs in the fossil fuel industry

   d. None of the above

3. Which two countries that emit the most greenhouse gases agreed to cap their carbon-emission targets?

   a. Canada and Brazil

   b. India and France

   c. Mexico and Australia

   d. China and the United States

4. What is fossil fuel divestment?

   a. An increase in spending on companies that extract fossil fuels from the earth

   b. The withdrawal of investment in assets from companies that extract fossil fuels from the earth

   c. A machine used to find oil and natural gas underneath the earth's surface

   d. A way to buy stocks and bonds in fossil fuel companiessurface

5. How does the cost of solar energy compare to that of fossil fuel energy in over seventy-nine countries?

    a. It is equal to or cheaper.

    b. It is much higher.

    c. It is increasing over time.

    d. None of the above

6. In 2016, how many people were employed in the renewable energy industry?

    a. 2,000,000

    b. 800,000

    c. 6,500,000

    d. 8,100,000

7. Climate change has caused humans to:

    a. Address deforestation

    b. Use resources more efficiently

    c. Invest in clean growth

    d. All of the above

8. Climate change mitigation:

    a. Reduces human emissions of greenhouse gases

    b. Is unrelated to greenhouse gases

    c. Is only done in Europe

    d. Doesn't involve humans

9. A building that is energy efficient can have:

    a. Solar panels

    b. Good insulation

    c. LED lights

    d. All of the above

10. In 2016, wind power:

    a. Was not used

    b. Witnessed a record growth year

    c. Was not a viable option

    d. Only worked in Chicago

Answer key: 1) d; 2) a; 3) d; 4) b;
5) a; 6) d; 7) d; 8) a; 9) d; 10) b

How What You Eat Impacts the Climate

How do your food choices matter to climate change? Just as our "carbon footprint" reveals the environmental impact of our everyday behaviors, so does our "foodprint." Its equation involves the amount of carbon dioxide generated to produce a certain quantity of food, the types of food (overlapping with the calculations for carbon footprints), and the amount of land required to sustain one person's diet. Other considerations: whether the food is organic, and if it originates locally or requires transportation from afar.

Some foodprint calculators test your knowledge of the environmental impacts of foods. Some consider the waste produced by types of foods. Some show how much water and carbon dioxide you can save by reducing your meat consumption.

For example, the BBC's "Climate Change Food Calculator" compares food items to other everyday human activities, including drinking water, heating your home, and driving. It asks, "How do your food choices impact on your environment?" Readers then select a food or drink and the frequency it is consumed to see the impact of their food choice.

The *New York Times* quiz "How Does Your Diet Contribute to Climate Change?" has users choose foods most similar to what they ate yesterday (for example, fruit and yogurt, bacon and eggs, bagel and cream cheese, or avocado toast for breakfast) and the frequency of some drinks, then compares their "foodprint" to the those of others.

For these and other "foodprint" calculators, go to earthday.org/foodprints-calculators.

Worldwide, Their Videos Tell Us

Around the world, videographers ages eighteen to thirty are submitting powerful short videos showcasing their local actions on climate change to the United Nations' annual Global Youth Video Competition. The winners attend the U.N. Climate Change Conference, but all short-listed entries are watchable via Geo-Doc, a multilinear, interactive database that situates the videos on a geographic information system map. No more than three minutes each, they provide a remarkable look at projects young people are working on worldwide.

From 2011 to the present, that fascinating map has each year added to its digital video archive, raising new voices of global youth involved in climate activism. The competition deadline is usually from late May to late July each year; to find out more, visit biomovies.tve.org or search for "Global Youth Video Competition."

Youth Action on Violence in Their Communities

High school students who survived the February 2018 gun massacre at Marjory Stoneman Douglas High School in Parkland, Florida, lost no time in launching an unprecedented national youth movement to end gun violence. Their school had suffered the deadliest school shooting in U.S. history, perpetrated by a nineteen-year-old former student with a semiautomatic rifle. Their Advanced Placement government class had just prepared them to debate arguments for and against gun control. Immediately after the slaughter, these youth took their grief and fury to the political arena—and the nation's media took notice.

March for Our Lives, their youth-led gun control movement, swiftly surged to national proportions. In the summer of 2019, its young leaders set out a "peace plan for a safer America" that went beyond the measures that lawmakers had yet proposed. Modeled after the organizing principles of Black Lives Matter, it effectively used compelling rhetoric, social media campaigns, rallies, marches, walkouts, and petitions. And it addressed not only school shootings, but also suicide, and domestic and community violence—the realities that youth were much more likely to encounter.[4]

Between 2002 and 2011, Black people were 2.5 times more likely than white people, and 1.7 times more likely than Latinx people, to experience the threat or use of nonlethal force during an encounter with police officers.[5] Between 2010 and 2012, Black males between the ages of fifteen and nineteen were twenty-one times more likely to be killed by officers than their white male counterparts.[6] By 2018, unarmed Black people (especially women) were more likely to be killed by police than unarmed people of other racial or ethnic backgrounds.[7] In 2018, police officers in the United States killed approximately 998 people.[8]

In the spring and fall of 2020, such community violence erupted into a burning national crisis of extraordinary scope and scale. Across the country, people took to the streets to protest the senseless killings by police of George Floyd and Breonna Taylor, as well as many other Black people who had died at the hands of those in power. The shooting death of Ahmaud Arbery, a Black man in Georgia killed by two white men while jogging, signaled the racism pervading U.S. culture. Countless media images documented police attacking peaceful protesters and journalists, and self-proclaimed white nationalists joined the offensive. When this book went to press, during the 2020 presidential election, political rifts were tearing the country apart.

The context of the coronavirus pandemic, which was killing Black people in greatly disproportionate numbers, only heightened the sense of systemic institutional racism. And with most schools still closed except for online instruction, angry and frustrated youth joined in the demonstrations even without organized support.

The drive for change has most effect when it begins close to home, Barack Obama pointed out in an open letter in the midst of the crisis. "The elected officials who matter most in reforming police departments and the criminal justice system work at the state and local levels," he wrote on his Twitter feed (@barackobama) and elsewhere. "I know the past few months have been hard and dispiriting. But watching the heightened activism of young people makes me hopeful. And if we can keep channeling our justifiable anger into peaceful, sustained, and effective action, this can be the moment when real change starts."

This section highlights youth who are turning alienation into action and offers resources to support that essential process.

We Are the Change Generation"

Lamont Satchel, Jr., seventeen, was a rising senior at a Detroit technical high school in the summer of 2020 when he wrote this essay, reprinted here with permission. It was published as part of Chalkbeat Detroit's weeklong Student Takeover (detroit.chalkbeat.org), which elevated the voices of that city's youth at a pivotal moment in America.

The death of George Floyd in Minnesota has felt like the final straw for my community.

The number of cases of police brutality against African Americans is overwhelming. As a young Black man, it sickens me and makes me think my life doesn't matter in this country. That thought process is dehumanizing, and trains you to lower the value of your existence and presence.

Now, Black youth in Detroit are taking a stand for our community and our existence. These protests represent our anger and frustration with a system that continues to fail Black and brown people.

We no longer want to live in fear of the individuals who take an oath to protect and serve us, but instead treat us like wild animals and kill us without punishment. Growing up as a young Black man, I have had to educate myself about how to respond "properly" to police misconduct during a traffic stop or arrest. Why should Black youth have to be taught how to respond to an unjust traffic stop or arrest so they don't end up killed? Why should Black youth have to be taught the "proper" way to reach for an identification card?

I've seen school police officers handcuff students and use other harsh, physical tactics. My peers have told me similar stories of conflicts between students and police. That's not the right way to handle these situations. We're just kids. We're still growing. Police shouldn't respond to us with violence.

We are growing up in a society where we have to adapt to misconduct at the hand of a police officer, instead of being able to trust law enforcement to handle situations appropriately. This country lacks accountability for police officers who escalate neutral situations. This is the problem.

As I watch my community protest and plead for respect for our existence, it motivates me. Black Detroit youth are doing everything in our power to support this movement. The majority of us don't want to risk leaving the house and infecting our parents during the COVID-19 pandemic, so we are taking our thoughts to social media.

I share stories on my Instagram and Twitter accounts to highlight the fight against racism. I've seen so many youth write online posts offering protestors care packages.

When we see a company that doesn't support our movement, I encourage my friends to stop supporting them. That's how we show our power to influence change. If your company doesn't stand with Black and brown communities, we, as youth, don't stand with you.

We will no longer stand on the sidelines and watch our people be abused and mistreated. It's emotionally crippling for Black teenagers like myself to feel that our lives are not valued, respected, or cherished. I want to grow up in a society and environment that can accept me for who I am without ridicule, fear, or a negative stereotype pinned to my back.

During school, we always used to hear adults tell us we are the generation of change. That statement holds more value now than ever before.

Trading Chains for a Leash

Saida Dahir, seventeen, grew up in Salt Lake City, Utah, after coming to the United States as a child refugee. An African American and a Muslim, she began writing and recording spoken-word poetry on social and political themes in eighth grade. She wrote this poem (reprinted here with permission) during the nationwide May 2020 Black Lives Matter uprising against police and community violence that targeted people of color.

> When a white man cries the world fills with grief,
> When a brown man cries the world's mourning is brief.
> When a white man cries the world weeps alongside,
> When a brown man cries they just push it aside.
> Our stories are hidden and there's nothing to say,
> We're a subtitle, they're the whole cover page.
> Their history is preserved, ours forgotten and aged.
> Their achievements are published while ours are backstaged.
> They are free birds, we're stuck in ropes and a cage.
> People here get ripped out of their homes by the police,
> We traded our chains for a different kind of leash,
> Afraid for our brother sister nephew and niece.
> Oh but kidnapping children will lead to world peace?
> What kind of bullshit is that, your "religion" chitchat,
> As if my struggles are one-sided, empty, and flat.
> You say go back to your country, go back to your land,

Our people have been beaten and broken and banned.

Did history repeat when they elected that man?

So tell me, are my struggles not justified:

How many children do we have to watch die?

Tell me, are my struggles not justified:

Immigrants killed daily as we watch and stand by,

Ripped out of their homes and their torture glorified.

I ask you, are our struggles not justified?

When will they see humans as more than dollar signs?

When will our struggles be justified?

We Are the People

In her senior year of high school in Oakland, California, Juliet Jackson wrote and delivered this speech as a culminating activity in English language arts.

When you're younger, police are superheroes, but they end up being the villains. They use excessive force and are not thoughtful of their actions as an incident is occurring. Once they tried to save my aunt from her abusve ex-boyfriend, and they just made everything worse. If only they had listened to my aunt, when she called repeatedly to ask for a restraining order.

The system constantly puts people in jail for petty crimes for long, harsh sentences. But police can kill an innocent person of color and they get a slap on the wrist and parole or probation, or lose their badge. They are supposed to "protect and serve." Why are they doing the opposite?

Oscar Grant was killed by police on January 1, 2009, after a fight that he was involved in on BART [rapid transit]. The BART police took him from the train and handcuffed him. Supposedly, Oscar wasn't "complying" and the officer "mistakenly" grabbed his gun instead of his taser and killed Oscar on the platform. The evidence, the videos, and everything the community had seen showed Oscar complying. In the end, the officer got two years. The average African American male gets three to five years for petty crimes!

This oppression has been happening for centuries. People of color are scared. Any sudden movements, our lives can be taken, just like that. In most incidents, the victim is cooperating with the police and they still get killed. Police need to be trained right, not to kill us off because of the color of our skin. Ever since the civil rights movement, we have been asking, "When will it end? When will we all be equal and come together as one?"

A Peace Plan for a Safer America

The same Parkland, Florida, students who organized and led March for Our Lives demonstrations after the February 2018 gun massacre at their high school spent the following year hammering out a comprehensive framework to address gun violence. Starting with a two-month bus tour in summer 2018, they gathered ideas from a demographically broad range of people in more than fifty localities and twenty states. For the next year, at least forty youth worked directly on the Peace Plan for a Safer America, through phone calls, in shared documents online, and face-to-face at a summit meeting in Houston. In August 2019, the student executive board of March for Our Lives released the plan below—not a legislative proposal but rather a road map for legislative action. Lawmakers "can take the parts they want," said Ariel Hobbs, a member of the group's student executive board, told the *New York Times*. "We're offering solutions to every single avenue of gun violence."

1. **Change the standards of gun ownership.** Advocate and pass legislation to raise the national standard for gun ownership: a national licensing and registry system that promotes responsible gun ownership; a ban on assault weapons, high-capacity magazines, and other weapons of war; policies to disarm gun owners who pose a risk to themselves or others; and a national gun buyback program to reduce the estimated 265 million to 393 million firearms in circulation by at least 30 percent.

2. **Halve the rate of gun deaths in ten years.** Mobilize an urgent and comprehensive federal response: declare a national emergency around gun violence and announce an audacious goal to reduce gun injuries and deaths by 50 percent in ten years, thereby saving up to two hundred thousand American lives.

3. **Accountability for the gun lobby and industry.** Hold the gun lobby and industry accountable for decades of illegal behavior and misguided policies intended to shield only themselves; reexamine the *District of Columbia v. Heller* interpretation of the Second Amendment; initiate both FEC and IRS investigations into the NRA, and fully repeal the Protection of Lawful Commerce in Arms Act.

4. **Name a director of Gun Violence Prevention.** Appoint a national director of Gun Violence Prevention (GVP) who reports directly to the president, with the mandate to operationalize our federal goals and empower existing federal agencies such as the Bureau of Alcohol, Tobacco, Firearms, and Explosives (ATF), the Department of Health and Human Services, and the Centers for Disease Control and Prevention (CDC)—agencies that have all been structurally weakened by the gun lobby. The national director of GVP would begin by overseeing a down payment of $250 million in annual funding for research by the CDC and other federal agencies on gun violence prevention.

5. **Generate community-based solutions.** Fully fund targeted interventions addressing the intersectional dimensions of gun violence: community-based urban violence reduction programs, suicide prevention programs, domestic violence prevention programs, mental and behavioral health service programs, and programs to address police violence in our communities.

6. **Empower the next generation.** Automatically register eligible voters and mail voter registration cards to all Americans when they turn eighteen. Create the "Safety Corps," a Peace Corps for gun violence prevention. The younger generations are disproportionately affected by gun violence. They should have a say in how their country solves this epidemic.

COMMUNITY POLICING

A Toolkit for Making Change

As police violence against Black people escalated in late spring of 2020, young people joined mass protests around the nation. The statistics confirm what Black youth know from experience: close to 10 percent of Black men in their thirties are behind bars on any given day, according to the Sentencing Project.[9] And incarceration rates for Black men are about twice as high as those of Hispanic men, five times higher than those of white men, and at least twenty-five times higher than those of Black women, Hispanic women, or white women.[10]

Urging both adults and youth to use community pressure to reform policing practices, Barack Obama recommended a 2019 toolkit that clarifies the actions such an effort involves: *New Era of Public Safety: An Advocacy Toolkit for Fair, Safe, and Effective Community Policing,* an initiative of the Leadership Conference on Civil and Human Rights (policing.civilrights.org/toolkit). These excerpts show how teachers, youth, and families can take action that makes a difference:

- By shaping public opinion through **organizing and advocacy,** you can influence lawmakers and law enforcement officials to change the way policing happens in your community.

- By **voting,** you can ensure that elected officials share your vision of public safety and are willing to take action to change policing.

- Through **service calls and complaints,** you can shape police priorities and document violations of rights and policies.

- Through advocacy and participation in **community oversight,** you can help hold departments accountable for individual and systemic problems and shape policy to prevent future violations.

(continued)

How can I change policing practices?

1. **Start the conversation.** Talk to family members, friends, and neighbors about policing and safety in your community. What does public safety look like? What needs to change? How can it be changed?

2. **Get involved.** Attend a public forum on policing, a community board meeting, a precinct meeting, or a public meeting of your local police commission or oversight agency, or go on a ride-along with a police officer. Find out what people are talking about and determine what changes you want to see. (*Note:* Information about local precinct or community board meetings can generally be found on the police department or city website. If not, call the city's general information line to find out when the next one will take place.)

3. **Access more information.** Find out about your department's policies and accountability structures. What data are available about stops, searches, arrests, use of force, and other issues? You can also research organizations in your local community that are already working on civil rights and policing reform.

4. **Speak out.** Tell your story and share your opinion. Write a letter to the editor or an op-ed in your local newspaper, or testify at a public forum to share your views about policing and safety in your community. Join the conversation online through social media and support online campaigns for increased police accountability.

5. **Organize.** Join an existing organization, coalition, or campaign—or start a new one!

Conversation-Starters on Gun Violence

Strong emotions often arise in conversations about firearms, as people recall their own positive or negative experiences with guns. Looking up relevant data from reputable sources beforehand can help lay the groundwork for an evidence-based discussion. When people's opinions clash, documenting areas of agreement promotes civility. Some starting points for such discussion follow.

- Rates of gun violence vary widely from state to state, as does the character of that violence. Comparing state-by-state "fatal injury data" collected yearly by the Centers for Disease Control and Prevention makes an interesting exercise, since it varies so widely across the United States.

- Gunfire has overtaken car accidents as one of the leading killers of young people in the United States, second only to drug overdose. Following decades of advocacy and policymaking to make automobiles and driving safer, the number of young people killed in car accidents has steadily declined. In contrast, gun deaths among young people have risen during years of relative inaction to reduce U.S. gun violence. The website of the Gun Violence Archive (gunviolencearchive.org) updates those statistics daily, year by year. In the year 2019, 3,068 youth ages twelve to seventeen were killed or injured with a gun.[11] Anyone can track the latest reports.

- The presence of a gun in a domestic violence situation increases the risk of homicides against women by 500 percent. Young women in abusive relationships face a substantial risk by partners or family members with access to guns. From 2006 to 2015, 36 percent of murders of young women between the ages of fifteen and twenty-nine were committed by an intimate partner or family member, and 54 percent of those murders were committed with a gun.

Talking Together About Guns and Gun Violence

Students take on differing perspectives on the subject of guns and gun violence in a substantive "town hall" simulation designed by the nonprofit Classroom Law Project (classroomlaw.org), in Portland, Oregon. As well as setting up the half-day project, its materials help students build their understanding of the beliefs of those they may oppose, including the following.

- Role descriptions for the different participants:
  - Rural resident (pro gun rights)
  - Gun store owner (pro gun rights)
  - Sportswoman (pro gun rights)
  - Sociologist (neutral)
  - Medical researcher (neutral)
  - Urban mayor (pro gun control)
  - Emergency room radiologist (pro gun control)
  - Exchange student (pro gun control)

- The text of the Second Amendment to the U.S. Constitution

- Statistics and research resources on gun ownership

- Links to current gun laws and policies

- A list of possible gun policies

- A case review of *District of Columbia v. Heller* (2008, U.S. Supreme Court)

- Gun policies and regulations in Oregon

- A review of types of guns

Youth Action on Voter Engagement

Who currently votes in U.S. elections, and why? Who can vote but doesn't, and why not? Who can't vote, and is that fair? If voting by young people increased, what difference would it make?

People between the ages eighteen and twenty-nine make up 40 percent of the potential U.S. electorate, but they have never voted in comparable numbers to older voters. That picture began to change, however, as youth activism gained momentum at the turn of the millennium. Both the 2016 and 2018 elections saw historic turnout in that age group. By 2020, 22 million U.S. teenagers were turning eighteen, and young voters were influencing the outcome of key races.

Teachers and other adult allies have joined the effort to strengthen youth participation in politics. Many schools now register (or preregister) students to vote, and the National Conference of State Legislatures provides step-by-step advice on how to do that.

The Center for Information and Research on Civic Learning and Engagement (CIRCLE), based at Tufts University, curates a wealth of resources for both youth and educators. Among other empowering projects, it identifies states and congressional districts where youth could have a disproportionately high electoral impact in midterm and presidential elections. As the 2020 election season began, the center was closely charting and analyzing a marked rise in the youth vote. And high school students around the country—like Brian Kur and Riya Mehta, who describe their political activities below—played a part in making that happen.

Many educators have come to see civics education as an ecosystem, in which school, family, and communities share responsibility for civic learning, engagement, and expression. The Democratic Knowledge Project at Harvard University names four outcomes that can result from that approach: civic knowledge, civic skills, civic dispositions, and civic capacities.

Teachers with those goals in mind often "start small"—perhaps with a classroom unit or an after-school club. Some join forces with local youth groups, many of which have launched or sharpened their civic focus since 2016. For example, the grassroots organization YVote (yvoteny.org) began in 2017 to build political knowledge and skills among diverse youth from dozens of New York City high schools. Several of the activities in this section come from YVote's summer and after-school programming; like many other civic groups, it also partners with schools to build capacity.

YVote has a larger national partner, Next Generation Politics (nextgenpolitics. org), which helps young people grapple with complex civic issues and current events. It brings "civic fellows" from area high schools to events where they learn from experts and each other, with other youth livestreaming from a distance. In student-led deliberations, small groups consider a particular civic challenge from multiple perspectives, then propose a way to address it through action.

At one such forum, participants reviewed the history of voting rights. Next, they examined seven different initiatives (such as automatic voter registration, lowering the voting age, and open primaries) that aim to increase the number of young voters. Using ranked-choice voting, they crafted a "youth voting rights" platform to present a few weeks later at a conference in their state capital.

In the world of politics, experiences like these build both capacity and confidence. Youth who learned about voting beforehand, for example, reported to CIRCLE that their likelihood of voting at eighteen had increased by 40 percent. This section offers materials to bring youth into the civic conversations that could change the political landscape for years to come.

Going to the Next Door

In the winter of 2020, at seventeen, Brian Kur was actively canvassing voters in Phoenix, Arizona, on behalf of the primary campaign of Democratic presidential candidate Bernie Sanders.

It's a mistake to try to force young people to vote just for the sake of voting. I think that the best way to get people to vote is to give them something to vote for! The youth, even conservative youth, overwhelmingly care about climate change. If you run a candidate who says he's going to be a climate change hardliner, young people will vote for him. I think it's as simple as that.

Canvassing, I'm usually part of a group of about twenty. I drive, so I pick up some of my younger friends and we go downtown where there's more foot traffic. We'll be the youngest ones, with some retired folks and some young adults whose job this is. We all meet up and say hi, then get our assignments and split off. The field organizers use a cool app called MiniVAN to send us to different streets and houses. It's a really streamlined system that uses names, addresses, and party affiliations from the public record. Afterward, we talk about how it went, go for lunch, and discuss what we're going to do next.

People are a lot less angry and resistant when you show up at their door, as opposed to when you call them. When you're on the phone, people have this implicit understanding that they can get angry without feeling bad about it, because you're calling them and asking for money during their day. But when you come to the door, people are more likely to at least act respectful—if they don't want you there, they will close the door. Usually they don't insult you or make fun of you, but if people are obnoxious, you don't take the bait—I pride myself on that. At some point you have to just walk away.

You do have to say right at the start who you're canvassing for. But you don't want to be in their face talking about a candidate before you establish the connection. I ask a few scripted questions, like "Are you happy with your health care?" or "Are you concerned about climate?" Based on their answers, I engage with people through a policy or a platform—something that actually affects people's lives. For elderly and disabled people, sometimes it's Medicare for All. For young people, it's overwhelmingly the Green New Deal.

You never argue, I'll tell you that. I am very much an arguer, and I had to unlearn that. Even if you actually find their viewpoint *bad,* they believe what they believe for a reason. And you can't change it by just telling them they're wrong. At their door, it's not your job to convince, it's your job to inform. Instead of trying to draw them to a certain conclusion, you can give them literature and pamphlets with information they maybe didn't have before.

The best way to get people to vote is to give them something to vote for. As a canvasser, it's exciting when people go, "Oh I didn't realize that! That's really interesting!" Even if they don't support your candidate, it's really cool. That's what keeps me going.

The most discouraging days are not the ones that get argumentative and heated, but the cold, slow days when people don't answer the door. I've seen metal shutters go over doors when canvassers come near. I've seen attack dogs chained up to fences. Sometimes you go to ten, fifteen, twenty doors before someone opens the door and listens—and that person might not even be predisposed to come over to your side. In a successful day of canvassing, you might talk to eight or nine people, but you've gone to more than fifty doors that didn't open. It's an uneasy feeling, not know-ing where those people are going to go politically. And it's frustrating that you had no bearing on that.

A big tenet of the Sanders campaign is "Fight for someone you don't know." Sometimes that can mean fighting for someone who acts negative or mean or rude or derisive or hateful to you. They are not your enemy. They are people who have a different view than you. When you have that viewpoint, you start to view your interaction as less of a confrontation and as more of a preface.

I do post on Twitter because it's fun, and it's interesting to get different perspectives. But I don't think my voice is heard at all on Twitter! It's a hobby for me, I'm not tweeting to raise awareness. People who think that activism amounts to posting on social media, they need to reassess their political strategy and their desire to do work.

My favorite aspect of the Sanders movement is "Not me, us." The work doesn't end with the results of the election. It never ends. Even if we achieve everything we want to, there will be more candidates to elect, work to do, policies to enact. I keep going out to canvass because I believe that the best way to defeat an enemy is to make them your friend. And I believe that the best way to do that is to make sure they never have to pay for health care again.

Talking Across the Room

Riya Mehta, seventeen, made political action a priority during her high school years in New Jersey. Before the 2020 election, she focused her efforts on voter engagement, and she explains below her commitment to bipartisanship.

I consider myself a centrist Democrat, but my political philosophy didn't really form until high school, when the 2016 election pulled me in. But at least a quarter of my classmates don't want to get involved. It's not apathy— it's a manifestation of an overwhelming political atmosphere. They don't know where to start. "People have very strong opinions," they tell me. "I feel like they'll start yelling at me if I am not informed."

I've participated in debate and Model U.N., and I'm definitely more moderate than most others in those clubs. But four intense years of debate taught me to associate political dialogue with winning or losing— not with bipartisan engagement. I really believe that everyone should have the ability and the encouragement to exercise their civic duty, regardless of what party they favor. That's why I founded our school's Bipartisan Club.

It's a weekly open forum, where about twenty students come together to talk about a controversial topic. We arrange the desks so the Democrats sit on one side of the room and the Republicans sit on the other side. As moderator, I sit in the middle and introduce the subject—maybe it's DACA funding, or the size of the military budget compared to the amount spent on Planned Parenthood. I might say, "Here's an interesting statistic that I found," or "Here's an article that I found interesting because it has a unique opinion on a situation." And then they just talk, across the room, one person at a time.

I don't try to regulate the dialogue, unless there's a screaming match or one person is completely dominating. We try for an atmosphere where good people can disagree. The goal is understanding—not "I'm right, you're wrong," but more "Here's what I think, and why." If someone objects, like, "I feel really insulted by that," then we pause the conversation to understand why that affects them so much. But if someone used bigoted language, I would ask them to leave, because our purpose is to foster dialogue, and offensive words shut down dialogue.

Not everybody has the same idea of what it means to engage in a civic manner rather than a partisan manner. All through high school, I've done voter engagement work with my local Democratic organization: phone banking, canvassing, and organizing others to do that. In an internship junior year, I worked with a state assemblyman on a bill to mandate offering voter information and registration to students in every New Jersey high school. But when I described that to an older person who works for the county Democratic organization, she said, "Are you sure that's a good idea? There's a lot of Republicans in your school, and we don't want them voting more than Democrats!" And more than one person told me that the bill would have trouble with the Republican side of the assembly and the senate, because teenagers who vote tend to be liberal.

The more you get involved with politics, the more you get hardened to that kind of thing. But I could never wrap my head around that mindset. It only increases partisan politics—and the very same people complain about how partisan our culture has become. In America today, we should be building the kind of movement where everyone has the ability and encouragement to exercise their civic duty, regardless of what party they are. Not long ago, New Jersey's Democratic senator joined with Utah's Republican senator to pass a bipartisan criminal justice bill. That kind of cooperation is why I'm engaged in politics.

A Current Events Carousel

Next Generation Politics (nextgenpolitics.org) created this group activity to help young people reflect on how political awareness develops, and how they could increase it. It is reprinted here with permission.

Goal: To gauge participants' involvement in current events—and encourage greater involvement.

Materials: Flip charts around the room; colored markers for participants to write on them.

Process: Participants post their thoughts about whatever current events they wish. Rotating through the flip charts for fifteen or twenty minutes, they also look at what their peers have written.

Large-group debrief: What do participants notice about what's written on the charts? Did they see any patterns in what people wrote? If so, what might those patterns imply?

Small-group discussions:

- What political news is on your radar these days?

- Where do you get your news?

- What does your *family* talk about, if they talk about politics? If they don't, why do you think that might be?

- What do your *friends or neighbors* talk about, if they talk about politics? If they don't, why do you think that might be?

What Gets Us to Vote

In the 2016 election, 40 percent of all registered voters did not cast ballots, according to the United States Elections Project. How did the turnout in 2020 compare with that? Find out the answer at electproject.org before starting this activity from Next Generation Politics (nextgenpolitics.org), which aims to generate youth interest and investment in voting.

The process: Working in small groups, students create three flip charts like those below. Thinking through the questions in each category below, they take notes. Afterward, they debrief in the larger group, asking, "What did we learn? What implications do our answers have? What next steps can we take?"

Basic Facts About Voting

- Who is eligible to vote?
- What does it take to register in our state?
- Why would someone NOT register?
- How does one actually vote? (In person? Early? By mail?)
- How do you find your voting place?
- What do you need to know, bring, or do when it's time to vote?

What we think we know	What we want to know

Emotional and Social Factors That Affect Voting

- Why would someone not register to vote?
- Why would a registered voter not vote?
- How do people feel about voting? What are their general beliefs about voting? How does that change their decisions?
- What drives an infrequent voter to vote? Why would they stay home?
- How do you find your voting place?
- What does democracy mean to voters? To nonvoters?

What we think we know	What we want to know

Physical and Logistical Factors That Affect Voting

- What about the logistics of voting make it challenging?
- How do people find out where, when, and how to cast their vote?
- How do people figure out who is running, what they stand for, why to vote for them?
- What do prospective voters need in order to feel prepared to vote?

What we think we know	What we want to know

Who Gets to Vote, and How That Happened

As youth learn the tortuous history of voting rights in the United States, they begin to see the ballot box as a symbol of equity and justice. At first, in most states only white male landowners ("freeholders") could vote. Step by step, others won that right: first nonlandowners, then Black men, then women, and then citizens who had reached the age of eighteen. The complicated story of how that happened involves both the federal government and the states—and the courageous political activism of ordinary people.

"Expanding Voting Rights"—a multimedia curriculum on the Teaching Tolerance website (tolerance.org)—brings that compelling history alive with videos from the archives of television news. The essential questions in its probing lesson plans, published in 2012, hold equal power in 2020 and beyond.

One lesson outlines new voting restrictions that many states instituted after the 2010 election, purportedly to guard against voter fraud. Noting the extremely low incidence of voter fraud, it asks students to examine whether those new voter laws aim to discourage potential voters who are particularly vulnerable for reasons of their age, race, ethnicity, language, or income. For example:

- *If they do not have a government-issued photo identification card.* Eleven percent of Americans do not have a photo ID. Many of those potential voters are Black, Latinx, young, and low-income.

- *If they do not have access to the documents necessary to take advantage of voter registration opportunities.* Some states require proof of citizenship upon registration, while others place restrictions on registration drives or same-day registration.

- *If they cannot vote the day of the election and need to vote early.* Weekend and evening hours for early voting have been cut back, despite these times being convenient for many minority voters.

- *If they have had a past conviction.* People with past convictions will find it more difficult to restore their voting rights in some states under new restrictions.

In the context of a worldwide pandemic, the 2020 election offers a fascinating opportunity for students to investigate what other factors might have a similar chilling effect on voter participation. For example, the incumbent president could use emergency powers to restrict voting in person, change voting rules, or hobble the postal service, all of which could have an impact on election results. State authorities could take last-minute steps to purge registered voters, close polling places, shorten early-voting hours, restrict voting by mail, or make other changes that would affect the vote. Voter intimidation by vigilante groups has previously shown a chilling effect on valid participation by minority voters.

As youth take up such problems of democracy, they are building the skills of observation, documentation, analysis, and civic participation. Their generation will sorely need those in the critical decades ahead.

Making It Easy for Youth to Vote

Voter registration programs in high schools make a big difference to youth participation in local, state, and national elections. In most states, school boards and districts can mandate that schools offer eligible students the opportunity to register at school or even preregister before they turn eighteen. Some states permit youth to vote in primary elections at age seventeen, provided that they will turn eighteen before the general election. However, other states introduced a host of confusing barriers that leave young voters uncertain about matters such as early voting laws and photo ID requirements. Useful advice that clarifies such questions can be found on the National Conference of State Legislatures' webpage "Preregistration for Young Voters" (ncsl.org), and in a high school voter registration toolkit on the website of the Center for Popular Democracy (populardemocracy.org)

To help address such questions, some schools now train "student registrars" to run their voter registration programs. Student leaders from community-based organizations have conducted youth voter registration drives in many states. Schools have incorporated material about voter registration in the required curriculum. Many schools have dedicated assemblies where students can register to vote, ask questions of local election officials, and see how a voting machine works.

Serving as poll workers during elections also brings youth in their teens into the elective process before they reach voting age, and almost all states allow that. In forty-five states and the District of Columbia, youth under eighteen may work as poll workers; in thirty-one of those, youth can start working at polls at the age of sixteen. Many schools give academic credit or other recognition for serving, as well as excused absences for Election Day.

Politics as Math

Politics may stand as the most important math problem that today's youth ever face. Numbers underlie not only voter turnout, but also the legislative process, campaign finance, the filibuster, and the census. Some assignments that engage youth in democracy's "numbers game" follow (adapted from the Education Week article "Math: The Most Potent Civics Lesson You Never Had").[12]

- Analyze twenty years of exit-poll results—including the 2008 and 2016 presidential elections, where swing states twice reshaped the national balance of political power. Indiana teacher Alison Strole asks that of her seventh- and eighth-grade algebra classes as they learn to read and interpret two-way data tables. The final task: Use that data to write a memo from either party's campaign strategist, recommending which constituency to target for a win. (Extra credit: Follow trends in voter choices through several election cycles.)

- Look for historical examples of the connection between math and civics (for example, the "three-fifths compromise," which for eighty years defined the value of enslaved people within the national system of electoral representation). In recent decades, college-educated men shifted their votes from Republican toward Democrat, while men with less formal education moved in the other direction.

- Analyze the statistics, graphics, and numbers that accompany new solutions and ideas in the civic sphere. Whether they apply to health care costs, plastic bottles, renewable energy, or inequitable parking tickets, these examples of the "social mathematics" or "quantitative civic literacy" skills will shape the world they live in.

Political Letters with Civic Value

"Writing a letter to a politician is about as 'civic' an assignment as we can do within our classroom," writes Sarah Cooper, who teaches U.S. history and civics to eighth graders. "And it feels especially relevant in our polarized political climate." In an article on MiddleWeb, she boiled down five elements that resulted in her students' "meatiest missives."[13]

1. **Go interdisciplinary with the topics.** Students designed, completed, and measured the impact of an individual Community Impact Project. Then, they wrote letters about a related topic. For instance, if they created a sports clinic for kids at the local Boys & Girls Club, they might write about what such organizations need from the government. Making public the letter (and its response) further increased its authenticity and impact.

2. **Base letters on a bill, if possible.** Students explored bills and articles related to their topic, via sites such as govtrack.us (for national bills) as well as the state legislature's site for proposals. They addressed its main points in their letters, as well as noting whether it had passed, or was stuck in committee, or fell somewhere in between.

3. **Find the best people to whom to address the letters.** For example, one of the two U.S. senators for their state; the U.S. House representative for the student's district; or their representative or senator in their state legislature. Other possibilities: members of the U.S. cabinet, or Supreme Court justices.

4. **Relate the project explicitly to how Congress and state legislatures work.** Working out whom to write and what to say, students start to figure out the

roughly parallel structures of the U.S. Congress and the state legislatures. As they understand what people in different positions do, they can ask for specific actions that help their cause.

5. **Give detailed advice and models for writing the letters.** The wide-ranging website thoughtco.com provides practical and realistic tips for writing letters to Congress in "Tips for Writing Effective Letters to Congress."[14]

6. **Proofread the drafts thoroughly.** Students might read and critique each other's letters. Still, it's best if they see your final assessment before they put it in the mail, having revised any problems of clarity or language.

Youth Action on Immigration

In an era when nearly 5 million English language learners constitute the fastest-growing student population in the United States, the multifaceted experiences of immigrant youth can shed important light on the national debate about immigration.

In the first half of this book, a number of immigrant students told of encountering hostility and stereotyping in their communities, even after they were speaking fluent English. But trusting relationships in their classrooms had helped them build resilience. "Little things are big," agreed two students from upstate New York—one an immigrant, one not—who recount later an incident in their Facing History class. In conservative rural Ohio, a white Mennonite student came to the same conclusion, as she tutored Latin American immigrant children and helped her church plan a support mission on the border.

Especially in the secondary grades, many newcomers face a double challenge: learning a new language while simultaneously learning grade-level content in that language. A leading edge of high schools—inspired by decades of work by the Internationals Network of Public Schools—have now prioritized the thinking and communication skills that matter most, regardless of the level of English that one starts with. In a supportive social and emotional context, students learn to use their new language to explore the critical issues of their time. In this section, a teacher describes how his newcomer class in Brooklyn, whose students spoke nine different home languages, created an ethnography of their very diverse school. And an innovative program embedded in a Lawrence, Massachusetts, high school has students practicing their English as they analyze the climate crisis that spans all borders. The Teaching Channel documents that work in its "Engaging Newcomers in Language and Content" video series, providing inspiring curriculum materials for English language learners.

Some contributors took risks as they told their stories here. They knew well the shadow of deportation that darkens the lives of roughly 700,000 young adults who arrived in the United States as children with their undocumented parents. Depending on which political pressures prevail, they might lose access to education and work visas. Many speak only English and identify as Americans; like their high school classmates, they have set their sights on a driver's license, a college education, and a job. But that crucial sense of belonging—the very foundation of a learning community—was shifting under their feet. If they spoke out, the door could shut on their futures. Yet their futures depended on others hearing their truths, and acting.

Changing Their World, Together

"We help students learn about hatred and bigotry so they can stop them from happening in the future," says the nonprofit Facing History and Ourselves, which began its work in 1976. Lorena and Ashley, the two young people who wrote the following commentaries, offer an example of how that happened—on an otherwise ordinary school day—when their Facing History class spontaneously pushed back against hate speech on the local airwaves.[15]

A SHELTER AROUND YOUR HEART

Who am I? This is one of the questions that popped into my mind as I was walking through the hallways after my first day in the Facing History class. I'm Mexican. I'm nineteen years old. I'm an older sister. I'm also Lorena, a student at a high school in upstate New York.

This will fulfill my self-portrait—what we call an Identity Chart. The picture we just saw—a student trying to be admitted to a segregated high school in 1957 and feeling alone and not wanted. I know that feeling. I came to the United States in March 2001. And starting a new life in a different country often requires growing a shelter around your heart. My experience as a new student was hard enough, but to go from a bilingual class to a regular one made it even harder. You never know when you can be teased, or even hurt.

But something about my Facing History class felt different. We were discussing the very things I was afraid of: being singled out and teased, stereotyping, neighbors turning against neighbors in history. The students couldn't react angrily to how people treated people in the past and then turn around to do these very things to me.

One morning, some of us heard a local radio station DJ say, "All immigrants should go home to their countries." The DJ began singling out Mexicans, calling them—calling me!—"border jumpers" and "wetbacks." I broke down in tears, and people were calling in and agreeing with him. In the Facing History class, we had been learning that little things are big—that moments in history, like the Holocaust, started with actions of hate. Our diverse class could have gone in separate ways or done nothing. But there, facing a crisis, we came together. We took the risk to go down to the station to protest. All we asked for was an apology. We didn't get one. I wish I could tell you that by going to the station we changed the opinions of the DJ and the callers. But I do know that it made us feel strong and proud of ourselves. Teachers and friends showed their support for our protest, and students who I had never met before were taking action, inspired by our example.

We learned from the class that changing the world can not always happen. But if you stand up for what you believe in, a part of the world can change. I have revised my Identity Chart since I took Facing History. Of course, I'm still a Mexican immigrant, a student, an older sister. But now I have added one word: an activist.

HISTORY, AND OURSELVES

My name is Ashley. I took Facing History and Ourselves with Lorena at our school. When our teacher came into the classroom in May to tell us what he had heard on the radio station, it set off a reaction. This was not the first day of class. If it had been, I'm not sure how we would have reacted. But having heard in class how people sat by and did nothing in moments like the Holocaust and the genocide in Rwanda, we knew we could not be like them. Me and my friend, half joking around, said, "Let's go there. Let's protest. Let's make a difference." Almost our entire class went to the radio station that day.

There's a quote: "Justice will not come to Athens until those who are not injured are as indignant as those who are." This course helped us all understand that. Justice could only come if we who are not immigrants were as angry about such closed-minded comments as Lorena was. All of us come from somewhere else. My grandmother was an immigrant. She came from England. But before she did, she watched her home being bombed during World War Two. One day she came into our class to share her story. My fellow students sat in rapt attention.

That's what almost every day was like, in this class. It was about how history taught us about ourselves, and how looking at ourselves taught us about history. What we learned from the radio incident, and from my grandmother, is that it is not just about walking in someone's shoes, about feeling sorry for them. It's about knowing how it feels when others who can do something do nothing.

One Student Works to Understand

In rural Ohio, during her last two years of high school, Danielle Novak worked on two very different projects to help immigrants from Latin America.

Many immigrants today leave their home countries to escape conflict, just like both sides of my family did when they came to America. My dad's parents immigrated here from Slovenia in the early 1950s, to escape oppression—and before college, I'm actually going to live for four months in Slovenia to experience the culture, meet the relatives, and learn the language. My mom's family were Mennonite pacifists who came here to Ohio from Switzerland in the mid-1800s to start a farming community. Like my mother, I am Mennonite, but I imagine most Mennonites are more on the conservative side of politics than our church is.

When I started tutoring English to children through a county Migrant Education Center, I got the sense that most of the staff in the program didn't have the same political beliefs and ideologies as mine. I expected that, being more conservative, they would not be interested in helping these migrant children. Working with those adults, however, I quickly learned that I was making assumptions. Everyone there was very caring and open, and passionate about what they were doing. They did not seem to bring in any prejudices. All of us would greet the students with high fives as they came in on the buses. When we talked at lunch, it would be about the students and what we could do to help them.

This was a summer program during regular school hours, 8 a.m. to 3 p.m. Some of the kids were coming from pretty far away—forty-five minutes or even longer. Their backgrounds varied quite a bit; some were born and grew up here, but others had immigrated here fairly recently. Some high school students had just come in the last few months and didn't know any English whatsoever. But I knew some of the elementary students from having worked with them the previous year. At that age, they're so rambunctious and playful, and they seemed really excited to learn. They loved playing alphabet games, and they had a really good camaraderie. Groups of siblings and cousins and second cousins would come in already with close bonds.

Especially when the young children were struggling, I learned that it's important to look below the surface of their behaviors. I tutored one very sensitive boy in third grade, who didn't have a lot of self-confidence. Many days he would come in to school very angry, not talking to anyone. He didn't have much of a language barrier, but he struggled a lot with reading and answering questions. I could see that he was genuinely trying. I learned to be very patient, not rushing him but helping him figure out the answers in his own time. One day after working together, he gave me a hug and said, "Thank you so much." I went out to my car with tears in my eyes! I was so proud of the progress he had made.

Doing this work has made me more interested in what's happening at the U.S.-Mexico border, because it's happening right now, in our country, every day. You can't ignore it. Some people see immigrants as faceless criminals. Another language sounds like gibberish to them. I saw these children's families, and they deserve respect. This past year, my church's peace and service commission has been planning a trip to go work on both sides of the Mexico border. I served as the planning group's youth representative, even though I can't go with them because I'll be in Slovenia. In Texas, they plan to walk part of the border, to see it up close. Some of them have connections with churches there, so they will help distribute food and water. They might go to an immigration court, to ask people there for names of others in detention. If you know the name, you can go and speak to them in detention and get them legal help.

It's always important to interact with people outside of your bubble—they have had experiences that you haven't, and it's good to learn from each other. In both the migrant education program and the church commission, I was a young person in a group of adults who had more knowledge and experience. I wanted to contribute, to accomplish something, and I didn't know if they would value my opinions and ideas. From the first day, I made the effort to not isolate myself from the adults—not feel like an outsider. I would eat lunch with them and ask them about their lives, and they would ask me about mine. They cared about what I had to say.

I think I did bring that youthful excitement and energy. But I was often unsure if what I had to say would help them, or just sound silly. Now I wish I had spoken up more, because I brought new perspectives. For example, my generation has been exposed to technology from a young age. It's a language we have become fluent in—and it's a way for people to connect and make plans together, or learn a language, or get things done in another country. That can make it easier for us to go into something completely new.

Young Ethnographers Study Their Own School

Instead of marginalizing students who are learning English as a new language, teachers can empower them with projects that matter to everyone in the school. Veteran teacher David Mumper, a resource specialist at the Hudson Valley Regional Bilingual Education Resource Network, described in a Chalkbeat article[16] how his class—students with nine different home languages and very diverse cultures—created an ethnography of their Brooklyn high school.

Some were native speakers of English; others, multilingual learners. Nearly all had experienced poverty, whether in Africa, the Caribbean, South America, or East New York, Brooklyn. What common materials and curriculum could possibly be relevant to all these students in my English class?

On the second day of class, all students found on their desks a personally addressed envelope, with a letter inside in English, Spanish, or French. (Those not literate in any language were paired with a classmate.) The letter invited each student to take the lead in creating an ethnography of their community. "I don't get it," I heard. "What are we doing?" By the end of class, students were working in small groups to determine exactly what the letter was asking, and how they should respond.

During the next class, we considered students' questions, starting with "What is an ethnography?" For students accustomed to being told what to do, the open-endedness caused uncertainty and silence. Questions arose: "Can we take pictures of the building?" "How are we supposed to find out about other kids in the school?"

Instead of answering them directly, I gave them space to shape the work, encouraging them to revisit the invitation letter and our ethnography definition. By the end of the period, students had decided to respond to the invitation with a letter describing their work plan. And they had brainstormed many of the roles and research methods that our ethnography would entail.

In the next few days, students drafted, edited, and published their "business letter" (usually a dreaded assignment). They also defined and chose roles: data collector, statistician, interviewer, photographer, editor, web designer. They were solving a real problem they knew well: how to welcome students to our community as they enrolled throughout the year.

In the following week, students worked together to create an orientation website: designing questions for their peers, recording and transcribing interviews in multiple languages, surveying the school community to capture quantitative data about their classmates, mapping their communities geographically, co-authoring and editing ethnographic vignettes, and curating and preparing their work for publication. Even as I assessed some of the tasks traditionally, student input continued to shape the work. For example, Amal observed that we could not accurately describe the community without including the adults in the school. In an important decision with an impact on our collective production of new knowledge, we decided to include staff alongside students in our ethnography.

In the end, the website project gave students space in which to consider their own realities, assets, and problems, and share them from a position of strength, advocacy, and agency. While they were developing content, students also negotiated identity and difference—not merely to become compliant learners, but in order to directly address their marginalization and reposition themselves as producers of knowledge.

Perhaps most significantly, I found that capitalizing on the diversity and strengths of traditionally marginalized youth can infuse discrete and isolated classroom tasks with new energy and creativity. Any educator in a diverse school could try this culturally responsive experiment right away.

In a Big School, a Scaffold for Newcomers

In a packed room, the elephant expert and the farmer were conferring on the perils of extreme weather, as the cameras rolled. The stakes were high, as they reached for the right words to convey their concern about worldwide climate change. But this conference on climate change had another high-stakes tension—its audience included not only teachers and high school students, but also a crew from the Teaching Channel, documenting a Model U.N. simulation for educators nationwide. And those playing the parts of United Nations delegates were ninth-grade newcomers to the United States and the English language.

"Model U.N. presents a structured way for our students to feel comfortable in academic conversation," said Joe Burkett, their World Studies teacher in the ENLACE program, at Lawrence High School in a Massachusetts city known for its immigration history. These language learners in "expert groups" were supporting their perspectives with research, then coming to a resolution.

ENLACE Academy (for "Engaging Newcomers in Language and Content Education") began in 2015 as a separate program within this high school of three thousand. It aims to serve the academic, social, and emotional needs of roughly two hundred ninth and tenth graders new to the country, and often at different stages of learning English. Instead of watering down the academic curriculum, ENLACE builds careful scaffolding for high-level tasks. A daily half-hour advisory period helps students deal with frustration through team-building, restorative justice circles, mindfulness practices, and current events discussions. Once weekly, different advisory groups come together to review upcoming campus-wide events and share their work, notes principal Allison Balter and her colleague Sarah Ottow on the Teaching Channel's blog, *Tchers' Voice*.[17] Their series "Engaging Newcomers in Language and Content" links to videos of ENLACE's curriculum.

Know the Rights of Immigrant Students

According to the American Civil Liberties Union (ACLU),[18] under U.S. law, schools may not

- Discriminate against students on the basis of race, color, or national origin

- Turn away students with limited English proficiency; the law requires schools to provide them with language instruction

- Deny undocumented children their right to a free public education or require families to prove their immigration status in order to enroll their children in school.

Youth Action on Gender Identities

The perspectives of lesbian, gay, bisexual, transgender, queer, and gender-nonconforming youth are increasingly emerging in the nation's schools, breaking long-held barriers against expressions of gender identities. Yet as these adolescents describe their experiences, they underline the pressing need for inclusion, safety, support, resources, and advocacy by adult allies at school.

Routinely, they hear their peers and teachers using gender-biased language. They encounter hostility, harassment, and physical assault. They feel erased by the curriculum and excluded by after-school activities. The emotional consequences mount up, and too few schools provide safe havens of support.[19] Even the bravest young people speak of how the powerful need for acceptance at school complicates the work of knowing who they are.

At one large public high school in Northern Virginia, students started a club called Courageous Conversations, to talk freely about issues often considered taboo in the classroom. The theme of gender comes up often, from unfair dress code policies to transgender youth's experiences at school. Here are some courageous conversation-starters the group has used.

- What do you feel is a taboo topic at our school? Why do you think it's taboo?

- Can you remember a time when you wanted to talk about something at school, but you felt like you couldn't? What did you think might happen if you did talk about it?

- Have you ever felt uncertain about how to talk about a gender issue? If so, how did you get through that situation? Do you wish you had acted differently? If so, how?

- Reflect on a time when you saw someone bullied or mistreated because of their gender identity. Did it happen at school, at home, or in the community? How did you feel? What did you do? What did others do? Do you wish that you, or others, had reacted differently? If so, describe how the situation might have changed.

- What changes at our school could create a more inclusive outlook on issues related to gender?

On a national scale, an extraordinary participatory action research project called "What's Your Issue?" has youth collaborating with adults to analyze the environments that queer, trans, or "gender-expansive" youth must navigate. An initiative of the Public Science Project at the Graduate Center of the City University of New York, the study particularly prioritizes queer youth of color, who are further threatened by racial or ethnic discrimination, immigration issues, or economic hardship. Its nationwide youth-generated survey gathered rich data about the dreams, desires, and priorities of almost six thousand youth, and dozens of youth worked with ten research cadres across the United States to analyze that input.

Strikingly, many young respondents did not wish to identify their gender from a list of possible identities. "I feel like I just exist," one wrote instead, in the space provided for comments. "I feel definitively not male, but I don't care to be female either . . . I am myself and nothing more." Another described themselves as "Everything at once, but also changing." One respondent simply wrote, "No thanks (agender)." Someone else wrote: "HELLA CONFUSING."

The project's leaders, Michelle Fine and María Elena Torre, point out a major demographic trend that the "What's Your Issue?" data yielded. In outsize proportions, queer youth of color are also bringing their energies to other social justice issues—police aggression, housing insecurity, unequal education, juvenile justice, health care, family violence, disability, and more. At the intersection of race and gender, they are finding their own ways to make change.

The efforts of those young activists are developing in different ways, and they have varying purposes. Yet all the youth who speak in this section about their gender identities—like their innumerable counterparts nationwide—make the choice every day to breach the barriers they encounter, in school and in the larger community. Their courage and honesty, and the actions of their peers who act as allies, do credit to their rising generation.

We Are the Salt of the Earth

Ashton Mota, a transgender high school student from Lowell, Massachusetts, stumped actively for the 2018 Massachusetts ballot initiative that now protects transgender people from discrimination in critical public accommodations. As a ninth grader in 2020, he spoke of the challenges faced by transgender youth of color.

> Growing up, I'd always thought about my gender identity. But until I was almost twelve, going into seventh grade, I couldn't find a word for the way I was feeling. When I came across the word *transgender,* that's when I came out to my mother. Even though LGBTQ topics hadn't been a conversation in our big extended family, I was blessed with most of my family's acceptance. My grandparents' first language is Spanish, and they really are old-school, but even with their strong cultural norms and beliefs, they were able to adjust and transition to using my preferred name and pronouns.
>
> I transitioned while in middle school, and at first it was really rocky. I was the first out transgender student in my school at the time, and the administration really struggled to support me. They didn't know what steps to take—like, "What bathroom is he going to use?" It made me feel like I was a problem that needed to be solved. That created a big pause, and I had been waiting too long to embrace this part of me. Today the school has a protocol and access to training, so I hope in the future they will have the tools to support LGBTQ students in a respectful and timely matter.
>
> My advocacy effort within the LGBTQ community started when I was fourteen. I decided to act publicly on Question 3, a Massachusetts ballot question to reaffirm a state law that protects transgender people from

discrimination in public places. I heard about it from my mom, who by then was involved with state-based LGBTQ organizations, especially those working directly to support transgender students. As November got closer, my mom said, "Ashton, this is an opportunity for you to use your voice on behalf of the kids who can't." That inspired me to do the activism work that I am currently doing. All LGBTQ individuals in the country deserve to have rights in the workplace and in public spaces.

The "Yes on 3" campaign opened the doors to many other platforms, allowing me to reach youth and families across the nation. Later that year I was invited to apply to the Human Rights Campaign, after one of their representatives heard me speak at a Boston rally in support of Question 3. Next thing I knew, I was serving as an HRC youth ambassador! It's a three-year term, and I'm now in my second term. This year, while attending the HRC's annual Time to Thrive conference on supporting LGBTQ youth, we lobbied on Capitol Hill. Visiting the offices of Elizabeth Warren, Ayanna Pressley, Seth Moulton, and many others, I talked about bills we wanted them to co-sponsor: a bill on the abolishment of conversion therapy, another that would place children in foster care with families that affirm their gender identity, and one about protections in school environments, especially in higher education. We talked about the Equality Act, which the House passed and sent to the Senate, which would amend the Civil Rights Act to include gender-related issues. When I'm home, I think and talk about this. But sitting in those offices on Capitol Hill—knowing that what I'm saying could make a difference—really touched my heart. That was a game changer for me.

Whether it's homelessness, employment discrimination, incarcera-tion, HIV infections, or violence, transgender youth of color continue to carry the brunt of the burden. I can only hope that when they see someone like me living life authentically—out and proud, transgender and Black—

it may spark a positive light in them. I did not have that before I came out, so for me it's really important to offer that to others.

It gets more interesting, because I am not just transgender and Black. I have many identities that intersect, and every day I come across layers of compounded discrimination, even within the queer community. For example, my family and I are Christians. My parents immigrated from the Dominican Republic and English is their second language. I am Latino, and I am Black, and when navigating those spaces I am often seen as too dark to be Latino, or not Black enough. And I also navigated white, elite spaces, as I attended private schools. I have always been seen as different, based on other's prejudices, racism, and classism.

I want people to know that I am human, and I have a good heart. We all deserve equal rights to live and exist. We need to re-center our conversations on humanity and treat each other with dignity and respect. Transgender people are not a burden, and we are not an issue or problem that needs to be handled. We are the salt of the earth and we make our communities better!

Figuring Themselves Out

In their first year after high school graduation, Wren Reeve took classes at the community college near their California home and also volunteered with local support groups for trans and questioning youth. They plan to specialize in disability, inclusion, and accessibility.

I was sixteen or seventeen when I started thinking about coming out. I used to attend a group at the local Diversity Center, specifically for LGBTQ+ youth who wanted a safe space to come and talk. At the time, I wasn't out to my family. I was just trying to figure myself out.

"Your identity can change and fluctuate," I remember the youth group supervisor saying to me. "But that's still valid, and you are still valid. People's identities evolve over time, and that's okay. You may not be the same person tomorrow that you are today, but you're still here." I really took that to heart. I finally was like, "I'm gonna do it. I'm gonna tell my parents this is me and this is who I need to be." I think it was a couple weeks later that I actually came out to my parents.

Now I actually help facilitate that group, on occasion. There is support out there—not just for youth but also for teachers, so they can start that conversation in their school. Local LGBTQ+ centers or nonprofit organizations do outreach for families and for educational systems. Organizations like Gender Spectrum and ACLU and Transgender Law Center have resources about laws in schools. And a lot of national organizations across the country, like the Trevor Project, help LGBTQ+ youth.

We think that kids are too young to talk about these things. But the younger that people talk about stuff, the more acceptance happens, and a lot less internalized struggle and mental distress.

Beyond the Binary

Asher, a student at a high school in Northern Virginia, presented this piece at an assembly sponsored by a student club called Courageous Conversations, which seeks to bring people together for structured, ongoing dialogues that examine the dynamics of race and ethnicity, socioeconomic class, gender, sexuality, ability, and religious identity.

> Non-binary: Not relating to either male nor female, a gender existing beyond the binary.

> It's a weight. A weight placed on my shoulders to pick one or the other. A weight on my chest and in my head.

> Weight that's more like pressure.

> You know, a pressure to present a certain way, like I'm being graded on my gender. Failing at acting and presenting how I'm supposed to. It's difficult to keep a smile when this binder causes more problems than solutions, but I continue to wear it because maybe they won't see me as a girl, for once.

> So like . . . What are you?

> Wow, that's a loaded question.

> Are you a boy or girl?

> Oh, neither.

> Conversation ends in

> Silence . . .

Like how I feel when I run for homecoming court in junior year,
but I am not accepted as a prince. Like how I run in senior year . . .

I'm on the ballot!

But they do not accept me as Ash.

They do not accept me.

Silence . . .

Like before the storm, the storm in which I finally correct people when
they say she instead of they.

The storm when I finally walk across the stage as Ash and not my
dead name.

Walking as me and not dreading graduation day.

The storm is this poem, can you hear me now?

Or am I just here waiting tick, tick, tick in your subconscious?
A clock you choose to ignore until the time for society's ignorance
is up because I AM VALID?

Alarming, isn't it?

To hear my voice, to acknowledge my storm because this weight is
unbearable. It cannot be lifted until school and society start listening
to me and stop placing me in a binary box.

I am a gift that comes unwrapped.

Presenting to the world as I wish and assert myself.

My name is Asher.

My name will not be silenced.

The Rights of LGBTQ+ Students

Schools often ignore (or even encourage) the bullying of LGBTQ+ students by their peers. Youth who experience this can seek support from the American Civil Liberties Union (ACLU) LBTQ Project, dedicated to LGBTQ+ issues. Its advice includes the following.

- LGBTQ+ students have a right to be who they are and express themselves at school. Students have a right to be out of the closet at school, and schools cannot skirt their responsibility to create a safe learning environment and address incidents of harassment.

- Public schools are not allowed to threaten to "out" students to their families, overlook bullying, force students to wear clothing inconsistent with their gender identity or bar LGBTQ+-themed clubs or clothing. Transgender and gender-nonconforming students often face hostile environments in which school officials refuse to refer to students by their preferred gender pronouns or provide access to appropriate bathroom and locker room facilities.

- Report any incidents of bullying or bias to a school principal or counselor. When that happens, keep detailed notes of your interactions with officials, and make copies of any paperwork that the school asks you to fill out.

To Change the Narrative, a Drama Exercise

As an advisory or drama club exercise, teachers might consider a version of the Brazilian director Augusto Boal's technique known as Theatre of the Oppressed. It developed from Boal's belief that simple drama exercises could help ordinary people find new ways to act and be, disrupting the oppressive forces in their lives and building community.

A youth group, for example, might start by writing or talking about experiences in which they either felt oppressed or acted as an oppressor. After sharing such memories (perhaps anonymously), the group chooses a few to act out as scenes for their peers.

To start, the "actors" play the scene as originally described. But then they start over, and this time other youth may "pause" and change the action, leading to a different, more positive outcome. After debriefing, the process may again repeat, as often as participants want. Along the way, they try out new perspectives on important social and emotional issues and rehearse positive new behaviors that will help when relating to others.

Video examples of youth using this method to address social and political issues in their lives appear on the website of PBS Learning Media ("Boal | Drama Arts Toolkit," pbslearningmedia.org).

NO MORE EITHER-OR

The Gender-Neutral Use of They/Them/Their

> If I have just told someone my pronouns, I'm not going to be mad at them for misgendering me. Even for me, it was a learning process—I still sometimes even forget! But when I've asked them again and again to use my pronouns, it's really frustrating. This is me, and you aren't respecting me and who I am. Some people just don't get that. They're like, "But you can't use they/them pronouns as a singular, it has to be a plural. That's multiple people, you're one person." And I'm like, "They/them pronouns have been around for a super long time in the English language. It's a grammar thing, look it up!" — WREN

Teachers who take the opportunity to practice, model, and discuss the use of plural pronouns can help others remember that neither sex nor gender is inherently binary in humans. Just as the use of *Latinx* offers a more gender-inclusive way to describe ethnic identity, and *pansexual* offers a gender-inclusive option to *bisexual*, so the use of *they/them/their* conveys the pluralities of gender identities.

English speakers use the plural pronouns *they* and *them*—as well as the possessive adjective *their* and the possessive pronoun *theirs*—to refer to multiple people, places, or things.

Yet since medieval times, English speakers (including Chaucer, Shakespeare, and Jane Austen) have also used those words as gender-neutral, substituting for *he* or *she, him* or *her,* or *his* or *hers,* according to Dictionary.com.[20]

Since 2015, the *Washington Post* style guide for copyeditors has approved *they/them/their* as gender-neutral third-person singular usage. In that same year, the American Dialect Society chose the gender-neutral singular *they* as its Word of the Year.

Just as a person who identifies as female uses the pronouns *she/her/hers,* or a person who identifies as male uses the pronouns *he/him/his,* nonbinary people choose *they/them/their* as their pronouns. Since those don't evoke the female and male binary genders, they also prove useful when (for whatever reason) one does not intend to identify a person by gender.

Many people use plural verbs with the pronoun *they.* Some examples follow. Try making your own!

> They are taking three honors courses.
>
> They have basketball practice at four.
>
> I gave them extra credit for the diagrams on the lab report.
>
> I watched their audition for the school play.
>
> They gave their lab partner their notes to check.
>
> I reminded them about their appointment with the college counselor.
>
> They asked me for comments on the draft of their paper.
>
> That jacket on the floor of the bus is theirs.
>
> They gave themselves time to clean the lab instruments.
>
> They gave themself time to clean the lab instruments.
>
> They wrote their final paper all by theirself.
>
> They wrote their final paper all by theirselves.

While singular *they* can refer to one person, it still takes a plural verb. For example: "They lead the singing all by theirself" or "They listen to a Spanish radio station on their way to school." (Some nonbinary people prefer using a singular verb with singular *they:* "They leads the singing all by theirselves," or "They speaks Spanish at home.")

When referring by name to a nonbinary person, you use a singular verb. For instance: "Wren takes two honors courses despite their busy schedule."

Acknowledgments

This book began with my friend Kristien Zenkov, a deeply experienced teacher and author well known for his "photo-voice" approach to drawing out adolescent learners. Now leading the secondary teacher education program at George Mason University, he suggested a sequel to the two Fires in the Bathroom "advice for teachers" books, which The New Press published first in 2003 (for high school teachers) and then in 2008 (for middle school teachers). A new Fires book, Kristien said, could build on those as it surfaced new issues that now confront both youth and their teachers. That made sense to me, but only if he, too, would contribute interviews and analysis to the project. He did that with depth and insight and enhanced the partnership by bringing in his colleague Meagan Call-Cummings, known for her sensitive elicitation of youth voices in participatory action research. We all owe thanks as well to Michelle Lague for her careful contributions in summarizing the academic research that buttresses the good work of teachers and their students.

We three co-authors would not have embarked on the work without the encouragement of my dear and stalwart partner, Barbara Cervone, who in 2001 founded our youth-voice nonprofit, What Kids Can Do, which supported the development of many books with youth. Barbara still keeps WKCD's archive alive and influential, and royalties from all the Fires books (including this one) go to sustaining that commitment. Her support has kept us on an even keel as we sought out and interviewed young people in very different communities and situations.

Those interviews also depended on a network of dedicated educators around the country who helped us connect with the youth they served. Each of us has far-reaching relationships with such colleagues in schools, after-school programs, and youth-based organizations. We owe a debt of gratitude to all of you who introduced us to the young people whose voices appear here.

In New York City, the generosity of Kate Burch, Steve Lazar, Frankee Grove, and Andy Snyder enabled me to spend many hours listening to their students share their thoughts. Sanda Balaban's network of YVote and Next Generation Politics yielded powerful interviews with high schoolers addressing the political issues of our times. Lori Chajet of the nonprofit College Access: Research and Action (CARA), a leading nonprofit, connected me with youth with powerful stories to tell.

In California, Eve Gordon, Alison Kreider, Kermit Pace, Lynn Lyster, and Sam Piha introduced me to the Oakland youth in these pages and lent important insight to the conversations that followed. Caroline Bauman of Chalkbeat helped me connect with Black high school students in Detroit who had powerful advice for educators, civic leaders, and their peers. The unflagging efforts of Montana Miller, a professor of youth culture at Bowling Green State University, connected us with individual far-flung youth who are engaging with the critical issues of their generation, and her BGSU colleague, the ethnomusicologist Katherine Meizel, led us to young spoken-word artists around the nation. Michelle Fine and María Elena Torre at the Public Science Project at the Graduate Center of the City University of New York shared powerful testimony from their ongoing research with youth across the nation.

Kristien Zenkov offers his thanks to the original Through Students' Eyes (TSE) students in Cleveland and his TSE project partners, Jim Harmon and Piet van Lier. With their pictures and their words, Kristien notes, "the TSE students showed us just why we as teachers and teachers of teachers should always 'ask first' and make listening to youths an everyday practice." If we learn to listen, he says, they will show us the way.

Meagan Call-Cummings acknowledges "the students who so courageously work for justice, equality, democracy, and peace in their schools, communities, and nations." She especially thanks the students in Idaho and Virginia who spoke with her and offered their experiences, ideas, and questions.

I owe my decades of documenting exemplary practice in adolescent education to my first mentor in that field, the late Theodore R. Sizer, who taught me how "essential questions" clarify and deepen learning. That practice must continue in these beleaguered times, and we have strived to provide examples in this book. We owe enormous thanks to the many teachers, school and after-school leaders, researchers, and teacher-educators who allowed us to include, or adapt, their insightful prompts and activities. The span of those friends and colleagues dwarfs the space we have available here; we pay homage to each of you.

For the past forty years, my most wise and forthright feedback has come from my close friend Laura Rogers: a gifted adolescent psychologist; a co-founder of the school we helped start with Ted and Nancy Sizer and many others; and my co-author for *Fires in the Middle School Bathroom*. Most recently, Laura has taught school psychology at Tufts University and served as director of its teacher preparation program; she read this manuscript with an eagle eye. Tufts has now named her a senior lecturer emerita, and I would like to offer her the same title. In countless ways, her insights illuminate this book—as well as my life's journey.

– *Kathleen Cushman*

Youth Contributors

Most youth who contributed to this book agreed that only their first names would appear. Where last names appear herein, those contributors made that choice because they already had a public presence. A sampling of their photos, provided with permission, appears on these two pages.

Adam	Ashley	Dylan
Adam Neville	Ashton Mota	Emily
Aissata	Athena	Eric Nelson
Alexza	Ben	Fatoumata
Ama	Brian Kur	Fowler
Andre	Carson	Hoda
Angel	Chloe	Ivan Garcia
Asher	Danielle Novak	Jeffrey

Angel

Hoda

Kaitlyn

Ben

Jeremy

Youth Contributors *(continued)*

Jennifer	Lindsay	Rekik
Jeremy	Lorena	Riya Mehta
Jordan	Maelynne	Rob
Juliet Jackson	Maggie	Rose
Kaidyan	Makiah	Rowdy
Kaitlyn	Marsela	Roxy
Kaliyah	Milan	Saida Dahir
Kate	Miledy	Saskia
Kaynna	Miles	Scott
Kyle	Monse	Shannon
Kynedy	Natalie	Shelby
Lamont Satchel, Jr.	Nyzja	Tanner
Liam	Reevan	Wren Reeve

Liam

Marsela

Saskia

Rose

Miles

Notes

Part I. What Makes School Matter

[1] Astead W. Herndon, "Black Americans Have a Message for Democrats," *New York Times*, May 31, 2020.

[2] The MetLife Survey of the American Teacher (New York: MetLife Foundation, 2001).

[3] Amber C. Bryant et al., "The Browning of American Public Schools: Evidence of Increasing Racial Diversity and the Implications for Policy, Practice, and Student Outcomes," *Urban Review* 49, no. 2 (2017): 263–78.

[4] Bryant et al., "The Browning of American Public Schools."

[5] Doris A. Santoro, *Demoralized: Why Teachers Leave the Profession They Love and How They Can Stay* (Cambridge, MA: Harvard Education Press, 2018).

[6] American Psychological Association, *Stress in America: Generation Z*, Stress in America Survey (American Psychological Association, 2018).

[7] Rebecca H. Bitsko et al., "Epidemiology and Impact of Health Care Provider–Diagnosed Anxiety and Depression Among U.S. Children," *Journal of Developmental and Behavioral Pediatrics* 39, no. 5 (2018): 395–403.

[8] Ramin Mojtabai, Mark Olfson, and Beth Han, "National Trends in the Prevalence and Treatment of Depression in Adolescents and Young Adults," *Pediatrics* 138, no. 6 (2016).

[9] Pew Research Center, *Most U.S. Teens See Anxiety and Depression as a Major Problem Among Their Peers* (Pew Research Center, 2019).

[10] Mardi Schmeichel, Hilary E. Hughes, and Mel Kutner, "Qualitative Research on Youths' Social Media Use: A Review of the Literature," *Middle Grades Review* 4, no. 2 (2018): Article 4.

[11] Schmeichel, Hughes, and Kutner, "Qualitative Research on Youths' Social Media Use."

[12] Philip J. Lazarus and Michael L. Sulkowski, "The Emotional Well-being of Our Nation's Youth and the Promise of Social-emotional Learning," *Communique* 40, no. 2 (2011): 1–16.

[13] Andrew Fuligni, "The Need to Contribute During Adolescence," *Perspectives on Psychological Science* 14, no. 3 (2018): 331–43.

[14] C. Kirabo Jackson, "What Do Test Scores Miss? The Importance of Teacher Effects on Non–Test Score Outcomes," *Journal of Political Economy* 126, no. 5 (2018): 2072–107.

[15] Elaine Allensworth, Jenny Nagaoka, and David W. Johnson, *High School Graduation and College Readiness Indicator Systems: What We Know, What We Need to Know* (Chicago, IL: University of Chicago Consortium on School Research, 2018).

[16] Allensworth, Nagaoka, and Johnson, *High School Graduation and College Readiness Indicator Systems.*

Part II. Five Briefings on What Youth Can Do

[1] Laura Tavares, "Nine Ways to Help Students Discuss Guns and Violence," *Greater Good,* March 7, 2018, greatergood.berkeley.edu

[2] Condensed from ACLU blog posts by Vera Eidelman, "Can Schools Discipline Students for Protesting?," February 22, 2018, and Brian Tashman, "Student Rights at School," September 1, 2017, aclu.org.

[3] MacArthur Research Network on Youth and Participatory Politics and the Digital Civics Toolkit Team at the University of California, Riverside, Graduate School of Education, digitalcivicstoolkit.org.

[4] Despite an uptick in the past ten years, school shootings account for less than 2 percent of all youth homicides in the United States. Kristin Holland et al., "Characteristics of School-Associated Youth Homicides—United States, 1994–2018," *Morbidity and Mortality Weekly Report* 68, no. 3 (2019): 53–60.

[5] Bureau of Justice Statistics, "Report: From 2002–11 Blacks Were 2.5 Times More Likely Than Whites to Experience Nonfatal Force by Police," news release, November 14, 2015, bjs.gov/content/pub/press/punfo211pr.cfm.

[6] Ryan Gabrielson, Eric Sagara, and Ryann Grochowski Jones, "Deadly Force, in Black and White," ProPublica, October 10, 2015, propublica.org.

[7] Gerry Everding, "Police Kill Unarmed Blacks More Often, Especially When They Are Women, Study Finds," *The Source*, February 6, 2018, source.wustl.edu.

[8] John Sullivan, Julie Tate, and Jennifer Jenkins, "Fatal Police Shootings of Unarmed People Have Significantly Declined, Experts Say," *Washington Post*, May 7, 2018, washingtonpost.com.

[9] "Issues: Racial Disparity," The Sentencing Project, sentencingproject.org/issues/racial-disparity.

[10] E. Ann Carson, *Prisoners in 2018* (Washington, DC: Bureau of Justice Statistics, U.S. Department of Justice, 2020).

[11] Jacquelyn C. Campbell et al., "Risk Factors for Femicide Within Physically Abusive Intimate Relationships," *American Journal of Public Health* 93, no. 7 (2003): 1089–97.

[12] Stephen Sawchuk, "Math: The Most Potent Civics Lesson You Never Had," *Education Week* 39, no. 16 (December 11, 2019): 1–12.

[13] Sarah Cooper, "What Students Can Learn by Writing to Politicians," MiddleWeb, February 10, 2020, middleweb.com/42277.

[14] Robert Longley, "Tips for Writing Effective Letters to Congress," ThoughtCo, updated October 2, 2019, thoughtco.com.

[15] Transcript of two students' video on the Facing History and Ourselves website (facinghistory.org/resource-library/video students-lorena-and-ashley-challenge-anti-immigrant-speech).

[16] David Mumper, "I Asked My Students to Tackle a Problem. Their Solution Taught Me a Lot About Culturally Responsive Teaching," Chalkbeat, February 4, 2020, nychalkbeat.org; condensed here with permission.

[17] Allison Balter and Sarah Ottow, "Building a Strong Learning Community for Newcomer ELLs," *Tchers' Voice* (blog), Teaching Channel, March 16, 2018, teachingchannel.com.

[18] "Know Your Rights: Students' Rights," American Civil Liberties Union, aclu.org.

[19] Joseph G. Kosciw et al., *The 2017 National School Climate Survey: The Experiences of Lesbian, Gay, Bisexual, Transgender, and Queer Youth in Our Nation's Schools* (New York: GLSEN, 2018).

[20] Much of this information comes from dictionary.com's "gender-neutral pronouns" entry in their Gender and Sexuality Dictionary, and "It's OK to Use 'They' to Describe One Person: Here's Why."

Resources

BOOKS

For teachers

Amy Burvall and Dan Ryder, *Intention: Critical Creativity in the Classroom* (EdTechTeam Press, 2017).

Jimmy Casas, *Culturize: Every Student, Every Day, Whatever It Takes* (Dave Burgess Consulting, 2018).

Lisa Delpit, *"Multiplication Is for White People": Raising Expectations for Other People's Children* (The New Press, 2012).

Christopher Emdin, *For White Folks Who Teach in the Hood . . . and the Rest of Y'all Too: Reality Pedagogy and Urban Education* (Beacon Press, 2016).

Fred Ende and Meghan Everette, *Forces of Influence: How Educators Can Leverage Relationships to Improve Practice* (ACSD, 2020).

Ibram X. Kendi, *How to Be an Antiracist* (Random House, 2019).

Season Mussey, *Mindfulness in the Classroom: Mindful Principles for Social and Emotional Learning* (Sourcebooks, 2019).

Ijeoma Oluo, *So You Want to Talk About Race* (Seal Press, 2019).

Beverly Daniel Tatum, *Why Are All the Black Kids Sitting Together in the Cafeteria?: And Other Conversations About Race* (Basic Books, 2017).

For young people (and teachers!)

Roxanne Dunbar-Ortiz, *An Indigenous Peoples' History of the United States*, ReVisioning American History (Beacon Press, 2014).

Sarah Lerner, *Parkland Speaks: Survivors from Marjory Stoneman Douglas Share Their Stories* (Crown Books for Young Readers, 2019).

Paul Ortiz, *An African American and Latinx History of the United States ReVisioning American History*, (Beacon Press, 2018).

Gayle E. Pitman, *The Stonewall Riots: Coming Out in the Streets* (Abrams, 2019).

Malala Yousafzai and Christina Lamb, *I Am Malala: The Girl who Stood Up for Education and Was Shot by the Taliban* (Little, Brown, 2013).

DIGITAL RESOURCES

Lesson plan resources and ideas

The websites below offer resources, tools, and ideas teachers might find directly applicable to their daily classroom routines across content areas.

Digital Civics Toolkit (digitalcivicstoolkit.org)

Facing History and Ourselves (facinghistory.org)

New York Times The Learning Network (nytimes.com/section/learning)

PBS Learning Media (pbslearningmedia.org)

Radical Math (radicalmath.org)

Read Write Think (readwritethink.org)

Teaching Tolerance (tolerance.org)

Staying involved and informed

These websites provide ways for educators to stay informed about current issues in education and/or connect to communities of likeminded teachers.

Chalkbeat (chalkbeat.org)

Disrupt Texts (disrupttexts.org)

EduColor (educolor.org)

Middle Web (middleweb.com)

NPR Education (npr.org/sections/education)

Rethinking Schools (rethinkingschools.org)

Teaching Channel (teachingchannel.com)

Teaching Tolerance (tolerance.org)

InformED (opencolleges.edu.au/informed)

Right Question Institute (rightquestion.org)

ThoughtCo (thoughtco.com)

Projects, organizations, and networks

Projects and organizations listed here offer teachers tools, strategies, and context to foster meaningful conversations with young people.

American Civil Liberties Union (ACLU) (aclu.org)

CIRCLE, Center for Information & Research on Civic Learning and Engagement (circle.tufts.edu)

Classroom Law Project (classroomlaw.org)

Global Oneness Project (globalonenessproject.org)

Critical Media Project (criticalmediaproject.org)

GLSEN (Gay, Lesbian & Straight Education Network) (glsen.org)

Harvard Project Zero (pz.harvard.edu)

School Reform Initiative (schoolreforminitiative.org)

#Follow this

The topics below represent online learning communities on Twitter that may be of interest to teachers who want to learn from and share ideas with others.

#CommunityEngagement (twitter.com/hashtag/communityengagement)

#EdChat (twitter.com/hashtag/edchat)

#EdReform (twitter.com/hashtag/edreform)

#EdTech (twitter.com/hashtag/edtech)

#EduColor (twitter.com/hashtag/educolor)

#GlobalEdChat (twitter.com/hashtag/globaledchat)

#StudentCentered (twitter.com/hashtag/studentcentered)

For engaging students

These websites may be shared directly with students to increase awareness of local and global issues and help young people become involved in their communities.

Change.org (change.org)

DoSomething (dosomething.org)

Educational Video Center (evc.org)

Next Generation Politics (nextgenpolitics.org)

PBS NewsHour (pbs.orgnewshour)

Science News for Students (sciencenewsforstudents.org)

YourCommonwealth.org (yourcommonwealth.org)

YR Media (yr.media)

For supporting conversations with students and families

These websites may be shared directly with students' families to provide tools for parents and guardians to engage in meaningful conversations with their children.

Better World Ed (betterworlded.org)

Greater Good magazine (greatergood.berkeley.edu)

NPR Life Kit (npr.org/lifekit)

Podcasts for professional development

The Cult of Pedagogy Podcast (cultofpedagogy.com/pod)

Google Teacher Podcast (googleteachertribe.com)

The Book Love Foundation Podcast (booklovefoundation.org/podcasts)

Flipped Learning Radio Worldwide (find it on iTunes, Google Podcasts, or any podcast app)

10 Minute Teacher Podcast (coolcatteacher.com/podcast)

The Creative Classroom with John Spencer (spencerauthor.com/podcast)

The House of #EdTech Podcast (chrisnesi.com/category/hoet)

Educators for Social Justice (find it on iTunes, Google Podcasts, or any podcast app)

Truth for Teachers Podcast (thecornerstoneforteachers.com/truth-for-teachers-podcast)

Blogs and sites for professional development

Cult of Pedagogy Blog (cultofpedagogy.com/blog)

Edutopia (https://www.edutopia.org)

Homeroom (blog.ed.gov)

Learning in Afterschool & Summer (blog.learninginafterschool.org)

MindShift (kqed.org/mindshift)

Teach and Transform (teachandtransform.org)

TeacherTube (teachertube.com)

Lisa Nielsen: The Innovative Educator (theinnovativeeducator.blogspot.com)

Index

anxiety, student, 2, 5, 6, 9, 17–18, 19, 22, 25, 87, 111
    coping with, 10, 25, 30
    See also depression; eating disorders; mental health; mood disorders;
        suicide
assessment of student learning
    via standardized tests, 9, 61, 69
    and student morale, 61–62
    with feedback on students' strengths and weaknesses, 70

belonging, student sense of, 19–33, 49
    in family contexts, 10, 11, 22–23, 48
    in gender-related contexts, 11
    in immigration contexts, 48–49, 148
    in religious contexts, 10, 11
    in school, xii, 17–19, 21, 27–28, 45–46, 89, 92
    See also community action; race
bias
    in civic issues, 104
    in issues of gender, 159–60, 166–67, 168, 169
    racial, and microaggressions, 42, 158
    See also stereotyping
Black Lives Matter, xii, 16, 40, 50, 62, 85, 90, 92, 118, 120, 122
bullying, 16, 18, 24, 39, 46, 106, 168
burnout, of teachers, 5, 7, 9, 14, 107

civic activities, for youth

    10 Questions to Guide Civic Action Projects, 97

    advocacy toolkit for community policing, 127–28

    analyzing factors in youth voting, 143

    "artivism," 106

    Climate Fact or Fiction, quiz, 114–15

    conversation-starters on gun violence, 129

    Courageous Conversations about gender, activity, 159–60, 166–67

    Current Events Carousel, activity, 138

    Digital Civics Toolkit, 104–05

    Expanding Voting Rights, curriculum, 141–42

    "foodprints" measuring climate impact, 116

    global youth video archive on climate action, 117

    Model U.N. for English language learners, activity, 157

    Peace Plan for a Safer America, 125–26

    Political Letters with Civic Value, activity, 145–46

    Politics as Math activities, 144

    preventing civic action burnout, 107

    student ethnography of their school, activity 155–56

    "town hall" simulation on guns and gun violence, 130

    walkouts and protests, 102, 103, 112

    What Gets Us to Vote, activity, 139–40

    "What's Your Issue" national participatory research project, 160–61

    youth action for bipartisan engagement, 136–37

    See also instructional strategies

civic concerns, of youth

    climate change, 108–11, 113

    community policing, 118–24, 127–28

    gender identities, 159–71

    healthcare access and equity, 119

    immigration, 147–58

    violence in their communities, 118–30

    voter engagement, 131–46

Claim-Evidence-Reasoning classroom protocol, 71

    See also instructional strategies

climate change, 2, 6, 8, 10, 73, 93, 96, 108–17, 133, 157

    anxiety about, 111

    classroom activities addressing, 111, 112, 114–15

    and "foodprint" calculators, 116

    and global map of actions, 117

    quiz on, 114

college

    access, 36–37, 51, 77, 78

    parental attitudes about, 20, 31, 74–75, 85–88

    readiness for, 7, 36–37, 72

    student attitudes about, 47, 55, 70, 78, 92, 144

community action, 37, 47, 50, 77, 78–79, 82–85, 88, 91–94, 100, 116–30,
       145, 162–64, 165

    in the classroom, 16, 27–28, 30–31, 37, 53, 61, 71, 91, 104–05, 111

    as a school, 21, 33, 73, 77, 155–56, 169

    related to youth identity issues, 10, 11, 23, 38, 40, 42, 44–46, 58, 160–61

crises, worldwide

    confronting youth in this era, xi–xii, 3, 6, 7, 14, 83, 119, 142

    learning from, 15, 60

    See also climate change; mental health; pandemic

depression, in youth, xi, 6, 29

    See also anxiety; eating disorders; mental health; mood disorders; suicide

diversity, of students

    and believing in ourselves, 16

    and sharing our stories, 28, 55, 162–64

    with teachers as bridges, 50–53

divorce, 19, 23, 27, 62

eating disorders, 22, 24

    See also anxiety; depression; mental health; mood disorders; suicide

English language learners, 4, 147, 148, 155, 157

expectations about youth

    regarding academic achievement, 12, 20, 87

    regarding careers, 85–88

    by parents or family, 10, 20, 22, 29, 83, 85–88, 90

    youth resistance to, 12, 13

experts, youth engaging with, 82, 125–26, 127–28, 132, 137, 145–46, 152–54, 160, 163

gangs, 17, 22

gender identities

    action by youth regarding, 11, 40–41, 74, 92, 94, 159–71

    and transitions by youth, 29, 88

    See also LGBTQ+; nonbinary; pronouns of choice; queer; transgender

gentrification of neighborhoods, 86, 91

governance, youth involvement

    in communities, 145–46

    in schools, 76–77

See also climate change; gender identities; gun violence; immigration
    status; voting
gun violence, 10, 73, 118–30
    and youth advocacy for regulation, 77, 93, 100, 101, 118–19, 125–26, 129–30

homelessness, 12, 21, 86, 163

immigration status, 14, 17, 49–50, 106, 123, 147–48
    and college access, 89
    and generational tensions, 74–75, 86
    and political tensions, 36, 65, 74, 76–77
    and school outreach to families, 23
    and students' rights, 158
    and youth identities, 12, 20, 23, 49, 65, 75, 164
    and youth as intermediaries, 12, 65, 74, 87
    and youth mental health, 12, 14, 17–19, 49
instructional strategies
    for building community, 13, 27–28, 53, 54, 68, 80
    for civic action, 84, 97, 127–30
    Claim-Evidence-Reasoning classroom protocol, 71
    for critical thinking and discussion, 15, 32–33, 35, 53, 54, 57, 80, 84
    "pair-share-square" discussion strategy, 84
    Purpose Gallery, 80
    Secret Switch, 76–77
    "snowball" discussion strategy, 84
    for student reflection, 11, 25, 66
    for writing and analysis, 60, 71
    See also civic activities, for youth

internships, youth experiences with, 75, 80, 82, 91, 100, 137

knowing students well
    to build trust, 26–29, 56, 58
    effects of, 9, 16, 58–59, 69–70
    through individual situations, 13, 16, 23, 33, 56, 58
    through their interests, 13–14, 58
    through their photography, 80–81
    questionnaire for, 56
    by understanding their challenges, 96–99, 102, 104–05, 138, 147–48,
        155–56, 159–61, 169

LGBTQ+, 11, 40, 92, 100, 162–63, 165, 168
    and hate crimes, 94
    See also gender identities; nonbinary; pronouns of choice; queer;
        transgender

media literacy, developing, 15, 50, 60, 71, 72–73, 90–91, 138
mental health, supporting students', 5–6, 18, 19, 23, 25, 30, 100, 126
    and youth advocacy, 100
    See also anxiety; depression; eating disorders; mood disorders; suicide
mood disorders, student, 5–6
    See also anxiety; depression; mental health; suicide
multigenerational families, youth involvement with, 11, 17, 22, 74, 82,
        86, 151, 162

nonbinary, 40–41, 166–71
    See also gender identities; LGBTQ+; pronouns of choice; queer; transgender

"pair-share-square" discussion strategy, 84

See also instructional strategies
pandemic, COVID-19, xi–xii, 7, 83, 119, 142
peer support among youth
    as allies, 23–26, 29, 39, 46, 47, 79, 84, 85, 102, 120–21, 136–37, 159–60, 166–67
    as peer educators, 78
political parties, youth engaging with
    bipartisan, 136–37
    conservative, 136–37, 144
    liberal, 38, 50, 86, 133–35, 136–37, 147, 152
pronouns of choice, 40, 55, 162, 168, 170–71
    See also gender identities; LGBTQ+; nonbinary; queer; transgender
Purpose Gallery, 80–81
    See also instructional strategies

queer, 11, 41, 159–61, 164
    coming out as, 92, 165
    See also gender identities; LGBTQ+; nonbinary; pronouns of choice; transgender

race
    actions concerning, in schools, 93, 120–23
    and belonging, 12, 39, 42–45, 46, 49, 62
    breaching barriers of, 47
    challenging expectations about, 16, 17, 37, 43, 44, 85–86, 92, 93
    conflicts and impacts of, xii, 42–45, 73

imbalance of, in teaching profession, 2, 5, 28, 45

statistics on, 4, 5, 127

See also Black Lives Matter; racism

racism, 16, 42–47, 77, 106, 119, 121, 164

microaggressions, 42

in schools, 43–45

in society, 40

systemic, 44, 121

religion, 31, 34, 48, 122, 166

atheist, 36

Catholic, 36

Christian, 11, 164

Hindu, 12

Mormon, 24, 36

Muslim, 10, 12, 31, 36, 40, 74–75, 86, 122

Secret Switch, 76

See also instructional strategies

sexual issues affecting youth

involving abuse, 74

involving consent, 74

education about, 40, 74

involving harassment, 6, 14, 42

involving health, 100

peer education about, 78, 126

See also gender identities

"snowball" discussion strategy, 84

See also instructional strategies

social and emotional learning (SEL), 25
    for changing needs of students, 2, 6, 98
    for communicating emotions, 10, 25, 30, 147–48
    competencies of, 79, 149–51, 155–56, 157, 169
social media
    as overwhelming to youth, 6, 73
    as political communication with youth, 79
    and students, 2, 6, 34, 44, 71, 90, 94, 105, 109, 118, 121, 128, 135
stereotyping, 11, 36, 40, 43, 62, 65, 92, 121, 147, 149
    racial, 10–12, 17, 36, 40, 43
    tools to challenge, 57
    See also bias; microaggressions
suicide, 6, 29, 118, 126
    See also anxiety; depression; eating disorders; mental health; mood
        disorders

teaching profession, racial imbalance in, 2, 5, 28, 45
transgender, 40, 159, 162–65, 168
    See also gender identities; LGBTQ+; nonbinary; pronouns of choice; queer

violence
    in the community, 8, 93, 118–23
    and guns, 100–01, 125–26, 129–30
    by police, 73, 93, 119–21, 127–28
    toward queer youth, 161, 163
    toward teachers, 5
    and teen dating, 100
voting, youth engagement in, 8, 94, 131–46